amigurumi
style
crochet

**Make Betty and her cat Bert and
dress them in vintage-inspired crochet
doll's clothes and accessories**

amigurumi
style
crochet

Make Betty and her cat Bert and dress them in vintage-inspired crochet doll's clothes and accessories

CARA MEDUS

Photographs by Jesse Wild and Ian Wilson

WHITE OWL

*For Granny and Nan, Marjorie and Margot, my
wonderfully creative grandmothers who would have
loved to have seen this book*

First published in Great Britain in 2020 by
PEN & SWORD WHITE OWL
An imprint of Pen & Sword Books Ltd
Yorkshire – Philadelphia

Copyright © Cara Medus, 2020
www.caramedus.com @caramedus

ISBN 9781526747273

Group Publisher: Jonathan Wright
Series Editor and Publishing Consultant: Katherine Raderecht
Art Director: Jane Toft
Stylist: Jaine Bevan
Photography: Jesse Wild and Ian Wilson
Production Editor: Elizabeth Raderecht

Printed and bound in India, by Replika Press Pvt. Ltd.

Pen & Sword Books Ltd incorporates the Imprints of Pen & Sword Books
Archaeology, Atlas, Aviation, Battleground, Discovery, Family History, History,
Maritime, Military, Naval, Politics, Railways, Select, Transport, True Crime,
Fiction, Frontline Books, Leo Cooper, Praetorian Press, Seaforth Publishing,
Wharncliffe and White Owl.

For a complete list of Pen & Sword titles please contact:

PEN & SWORD BOOKS LIMITED
47 Church Street, Barnsley, South Yorkshire S70 2AS, England
E-mail: enquiries@pen-and-sword.co.uk
Website: www.pen-and-sword.co.uk
or
PEN AND SWORD BOOKS
1950 Lawrence Rd, Havertown, PA 19083, USA
E-mail: Uspen-and-sword@casematepublishers.com
Website: www.penandswordbooks.com

contents

introduction

I have to confess, the idea for this book came to me because I still love the thought of playing dress-up with a doll, like I did when I was a child. Amigurumi crochet is perfect for making figures, so what better way to combine a love of crochet, with dressing up?

Crochet is so versatile that you can make it do things that you never thought possible. That's what I love about it. I love all the little details that make an outfit, or a figure 'just right'.

Let me introduce you to Betty and Bert the Cat. Betty is the image of the 1950s housewife, stylish to a tee, in her heels when doing the housework and when out shopping for groceries. Of course, she loves to crochet and all things crafty. She has her saucy side too, as you'll see when you peep into her bedroom! Bert is independent (what cat isn't?), but cheeky, and hopes secretly that he can be part of all Betty's adventures.

I hope that you enjoy coming on a little crochet journey with me, along with Betty and Bert. I also hope that it will bring you as much creative joy as it did to me in designing it. We all need to play from time to time!

Betty at home

Betty at the movies

Betty goes on holiday

Betty's boudoir

Betty goes dancing

Betty goes shopping

chapter one: the basics

Here are a few details that should help making Betty and Bert go smoothly. Have a read through this chapter before you begin and you'll get some hints and tips to help you create your amigurumi-style figures more easily

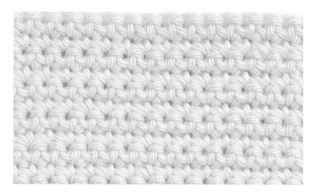

Double crochet worked back and forth in rows

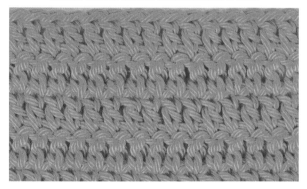

Treble crochet worked back and forth in rows

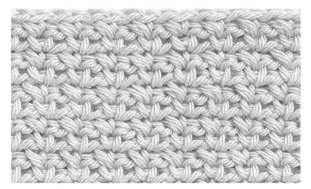

(Dc, ch1) rib pattern worked back and forth in rows

STITCH PATTERNS

Betty and Bert are made using the traditional amigurumi method of working in a spiral without closing off each round with a slip stitch. I recommend that you work these pieces in the front loop only, as this helps to line up the stitches more evenly and prevent too much 'drift' at the beginning of the round. This is needed to keep shaping accurate. It will help to use a marker at the beginning of each round. I prefer to use a piece of marking yarn that you can weave back and forth at the beginning of the round because it stays in place should you need to rip any of the work back to a particular position.

Most of the outfits are worked in straightforward double crochet/treble crochet rows. There is also a (dc, ch1) rib pattern that is used for the Skirt, Sheath Dress, Capri Pants and Baby Doll Pyjamas. This gives the pieces some stretch.

When working in double crochet in rows, or in the (dc, ch1) rib pattern, the ch1 turning ch does not count as a stitch throughout.

Double crochet worked in the round in front loops only

HOOK SIZES AND TENSION

A 2.5mm hook is used for making the figures of Betty and Bert and a 3mm hook for most of the outfits and accessories. The outfits have been designed to fit Betty at the tension given, so it's always a good idea to match the tension by changing to a larger or smaller hook if necessary. Your tension will affect the size of your finished pieces and the yarn quantities used. For the pieces that need stuffing, it's best to keep quite a firm tension so that it prevents the stuffing from showing through. The tension for the most common stitch patterns is as follows:

Double crochet worked in the round in front loops only: 30 sts and 26 rows to measure 10x10cm with a 2.5mm hook.
Double crochet worked back and forth in rows: 22 sts and 24 rows to measure 10x10cm with a 3mm hook.
(Dc, ch1) rib worked back and forth in rows: 27 sts and 25 rows to measure 10x10cm with a 3mm hook.
Treble crochet worked back and forth in rows: 22 sts and 11.5 rows to measure 10x10cm with a 3mm hook.

SKILL LEVEL

It will help to have some experience of crocheting amigurumi-type figures to make the items in this book. Most of the items have straightforward stitch patterns and construction, and I've given alternatives where there are techniques or materials that are more challenging. Anything very small is a bit fiddly, so for the shoes, the Ballet Flats on page 68 are the simplest to make. The Capri Pants on page 60 require the most concentration, so maybe don't try these in front of the television! You can choose whether you make Betty's hair removable, or whether you sew it straight to the Head, which is simpler. Details are given with the Hair in a Bun pattern on page 21.

YARN AND YARN QUANTITIES

Scheepjes Catona is available in 10g, 25g and 50g balls

Almost all of the patterns are worked in Scheepjes Catona (100% cotton, 50g/125m). Occasionally, Scheepjes Maxi Sweet Treat (100% cotton, 25g/140m) is used. Maxi is a thread-weight yarn, so I've suggested alternatives where this is used in case you prefer not to work with a fine yarn.

Approximate yarn quantities are given for each shade in each pattern, to the nearest 5g. These are only intended as a guide and quantities will vary according to your tension. The total yarn quantities for each section are given at the beginning of the section to help you determine the yarn to purchase, but you may also want to check the list of all the yarn needed for all projects, which you'll find on page 121.

PATTERN TERMS

UK crochet terms are used throughout the book. For a list of abbreviations and chart symbols see page 120.

A NOTE ABOUT DECREASING

The decreases throughout as 'dec' instead of specifying the decrease method. I recommend using 'skip next st, dc in next st' where this is stated. This is the easiest decrease method, especially when there are several decreases worked in the same place on several rounds. This works particularly well when using a 2.5mm hook as you can get away without it showing in the fabric. Occasionally another decrease method is used because it is more suitable at that time, and in this case, the decrease will be stated as dc2tog. In all cases, 'dec' uses 2 sts of the previous row/round, so if you're skipping sts, you'll need to read 'skip next st, dc in next st' where you see the instruction 'dec'.

LINING FABRIC

Sometimes the crochet fabric needs strengthening to give it a bit more rigidity. The method most often used is to stick lining fabric inside some of the pieces – the Handbags, insoles of Shoes, Bert's Baskets and the Eye Masks. I used two different cotton fabric prints, a

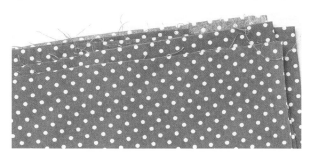

spotty one for Betty, and a mouse print one (Rose and Hubble Fabrics) for Bert. A piece about 25cm square should be enough for all of Betty's items, and a piece 30cm square for Bert's.

Prepare these pieces of fabric by adding a little water to white craft glue (PVA), so that it's about the consistency of single cream. This will make it easier for the fabric to absorb the glue. Brush the fabric with the glue all over on both sides and leave it flat to dry, stretching it to flatten it as it dries. Make sure you dry it on top of a plastic bag or cling film so that it doesn't stick to the surface! Once it's dry the fabric will be paper-like and easy to cut with scissors without fraying. You can use the same glue to stick it to the finished crochet pieces.

I've also used sticky fabric dressing tape on the reverse of some pieces where it won't be seen. Dressing tape is also useful for binding the ends of any wires used.

TOY FILLING

Polyester toy filling can be used for the pieces that need stuffing, although I prefer wool filling because it doesn't seem to take as long to compact. It's worth spending a little time on the stuffing, moulding it to shape as you work and filling the pieces firmly, as this will improve the end result. Plastic toy granules are also used where the items need a little more weight. Don't be tempted to use pulses or rice as a substitute as these degrade over time and attract pests. I've also used old pairs of black tights cut into small pieces to stuff some of the Bert parts, as the black doesn't show through the crochet like toy filling would.

For safety reasons, Betty and Bert are not intended as toys for young children; there are too many small parts and wires.

FINISHING

Double crochet fabric has a tendency to curl, and the finished appearance will be improved by blocking some of the pieces afterwards to flatten it. To do this, spray with water until damp, pin or stretch flat into position and leave it to dry. For particularly stubborn curling, or things that need to hold their shape, try using spray starch. Just be careful to avoid areas that might have been glued when wetting the fabric – it's better to block before adding finishing details for this reason.

chapter two: making betty

Making Betty in the buff is the starting place for all the other projects. She's got a fine pair of shapely calves and the classic 1950s hourglass figure. She needs a bit of help to stand up straight with hidden wires, which give her excellent posture

Total yarn quantities for this section:
Scheepjes Catona
75g of Nude (255)
15g of Chocolate (507)
15g of Soft Rose (409) for integrated bra and pants
Scheepjes Maxi Sweet Treat
7g of Soft Rose (409) for removable bra and pants
Black embroidery thread

Check the yarn quantities needed for all projects on page 121.

DOLL
Materials
▪ Scheepjes Catona, Nude (75g)
▪ A 2.5mm hook
▪ Black embroidery thread
▪ 2 small pearl beads
▪ Sticky fabric dressing tape
▪ 4 pipe cleaners, 30cm long
▪ Paperclips, 3cm long
▪ Toy filling
▪ Wire or foam covered hair curlers
▪ Stitch markers
▪ Wire cutters
▪ Pliers

See note about decreasing on page 10.

Measurements
Betty measures 35cm tall.

To preserve her modesty, Betty has removable underwear, but you can also make the Bra and Pants as part of the doll by changing colours as you work. You can make her immaculate hairdo as a separate piece to change the style to suit her whims or sew it in place if you'd prefer a low-maintenance Betty. If you need help making her, take a look at the tutorial videos on caramedus.com in the Betty and Bert section.

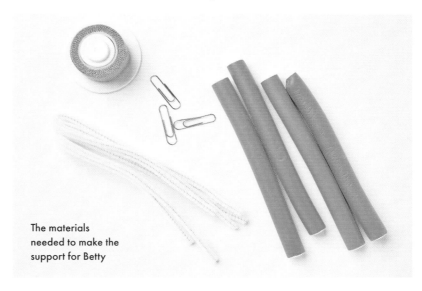

The materials needed to make the support for Betty

BEFORE YOU BEGIN
Support for Betty
Betty needs a bit of help to stand up straight, so she's made around a wire support. I used flexible foam hair curlers which are perfect for this purpose because they have the right amount of 'bend'; you need wire which will bend fairly easily with your hands but which will also retain its shape. The foam outer means that you don't need to use as much filling. The ones I used are 14.5cm long with a plastic cap on each end, and have wire inside with a small loop at each end (wilko.com). To stop the colour of the foam showing through the crochet, wrap them with sticky fabric dressing tape on the lower legs and the neck. You can also use sections of plain

wire instead. Make a small loop at each end of the section of wire with pliers. If not using this loop to attach to another wire, it will prevent the sharp end sticking out. The measurements given for each wire are taken after the loops have been made.

You'll need one curler or piece of wire for each leg, and the total length of each piece needs to be a bit longer than each leg from heel to top – approximately 16cm long. I extended the length of the curler by removing the end and putting a paperclip through the loop of wire. You'll need another curler or wire for the centre body wire, 14.5cm long. The arms are reinforced with pipe cleaners. The instructions for the wire supports are given in the pattern at the relevant points.

CONSTRUCTION

Work in a spiral without closing off each round with a ss and in front loops only unless otherwise stated. The Legs and Arms are made first separately. The hip to underarm part of the Body is made and the Arms are joined into the Body by working the round around the Body and Arms in one. The wires for the Legs and Body are put in place and the Legs are stuffed and sewn on. The Body is stuffed to the underarms. The pipe cleaners in the Arms are joined to the central wire before stuffing and completing the shoulders and neck. The Head is made separately, stuffed and sewn on to the neck.

UNDERWEAR

There are patterns below for removable Bra and Pants. These are worked with Scheepjes Maxi and a 2.5mm hook to reduce the bulk underneath other clothes. If you prefer not to work with a fine yarn and smaller hook, then you can make the Bra and Pants part of the Doll by changing to Catona Soft Rose for these sections as instructed in the pattern. The amount of Nude yarn needed is for working the entire doll in this colour, so you'll need less of this yarn if choosing

this option. If making the Bra and Pants part of the doll, you might find that they show at the edges of some of the other pieces of clothing in the book – the Swimsuit and Evening Gown, for example. You can minimise this by putting some shirring elastic on the Cup edges of these pieces to pull them in slightly. Otherwise, she can just go without underwear for these outfits, shock horror!

LEG (MAKE 2)

The Leg is worked from the bottom up, starting at the Heel. The Heel piece is worked in a circular fashion to 20 sts, and then the Leg is worked from the top 11 sts of the circle, and the Foot is worked later from the bottom 9 sts (see Heel Circle diagram on page 122).

The position of some of the shaping sts in the legs is indicated by their relationship to the centre front (CF) or centre back (CB). For example, you might be instructed to work 2dc in the 4th and 5th sts from the CF on the outside edge of the Leg. It's easy to find the centre front (and therefore also the centre back) of the Leg at any point by flattening it in line with the join of the Heel circle. This makes it possible to write the pattern for both legs at the same time, and doesn't depend on the 'drift' which occurs in the starting point of the round. If at any point the start of the round conflicts with the increase sts, undo enough sts to bring the start of the round before the increase sts.

Heel Circle

With Nude and a 2.5mm hook, make a magic loop.
Round 1 (RS) Ch1, 5dc into loop. [5 sts]
Work in a spiral in front loops only throughout.

Round 2 2dc in each st around. [10 sts]

Round 3 (2dc in next st, 1dc) 5 times. [15 sts]

Round 4 (partial round) (2dc in next st, 1dc) 5 times. [20 sts]

The first st of the next round will be the new start of the round.

Ankle to Knee

Round 5 5dc, skip next 9 sts, 6dc. [11 sts]

Rounds 6-9 2dc in first st, dc in each rem st around. [15 sts after Round 9]

Round 10 Dc in each st around.

Rounds 11-14 2dc in first st, dc in each rem st around. [19 sts after Round 14]

Round 15 2dc in first st, 9dc, 2dc in next st, 8dc. [21 sts]

Rounds 16-17 Dc in each st around.

Round 18 Decrease once at CB, dc in each rem st around. [20 sts]

Round 19 Decrease five times over the 10 sts at the back of the Leg, dc in each rem st around. [15 sts]

Round 20 Dc in each st around.

Round 21 Dc in each st around, with 2dc in 4th and 5th sts from CF on inside edge of Leg. [17 sts]

Round 22 Dc in each st around, with 2dc in 4th and 5th sts from CF on outside edge of Leg. [19 sts]

Knee to Hip

Round 23 Dc in each st around, with 2dc in 4th, 5th and 6th sts from CF on outside edge. [22 sts]

Rounds 24-25 Dc in each st around.

Rounds 26-32 Dc in each st around, with 2dc in 7th st from CF on outside edge. [29 sts after Round 32]

Rounds 33-35 Dc in each st around.

Round 36 Dc in each st around, with 2dc in 4th and 10th sts from CF on outside edge. [31 sts]

If the start of the round isn't already at the centre front, dc in each st around to centre front.

Rounds 37-38 Ss loosely in next 14 sts from CF on inside edge of Leg and dc in rem 17 sts from CF on outside edge of Leg, ss in next st, fasten off leaving a long tail.

Foot

Rejoin Nude with a dc at the join of the Heel circle, in the same st as the 5th st of Round 5.

Round 1 (RS) 3dc, dc2tog, 4dc, dc in same st as 6th st of Round 5. [10 sts]

Round 2 Dc in each st around.

Round 3 4dc, (2dc in next st) twice, 4dc. [12 sts]

Round 4 Dc in each st around.

Round 5 5dc, dc2tog, 5dc. [11 sts]

Round 6 (partial round) Dc around to the edge of the Foot, fasten off leaving a tail for sewing. You'll close the Foot once the Leg and Foot are stuffed.

To Finish Leg/Foot

Use the tail end of yarn at the Heel circle join to sew up any gap here. Now prepare the wire for the Leg. This needs to reach the base of the Foot, and extend above the top of the Leg slightly. Bind the end of the wire at the ankle with fabric dressing strip so that it doesn't stick through the crochet.

If using foam curlers, you may need to extend the length of the curler. I used a paperclip hooked into the end of the wire inside the curlers.

Trim the foam around the curlers so that it tapers for

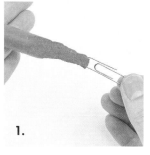
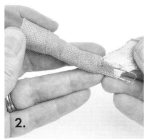

the ankle {1}, and bind the trimmed end of the curler and the paperclip with fabric dressing strip so that the paperclip is completely enclosed {2}.

With the wire in place, stuff the Leg from the top,

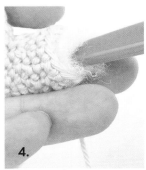

pushing a little filling carefully beyond the knee into the calf **{3}**. Stuff the Foot from the Foot end **{4}**. Use the tail end of yarn at the Foot to sew the end of the Foot closed.

ARM (MAKE 2)
Make the Thumb of the Hand separately and sew it on afterwards.

Thumb
With Nude and a 2.5mm hook, ch3.
Row 1 (RS) Dc in second ch from hook and next ch, turn. [2 sts]
Row 2 Ch1, ss both the front loop and the foundation ch loop of the first st together. Repeat for second st. If it's difficult to get the hook into this st, try using a finer metal hook. Ss into end of row (forms top of Thumb), fasten off and thread the tail of yarn down through the Thumb.

Hand
With Nude and a 2.5mm hook, make a magic loop. Work in a spiral in front loops only throughout.
Round 1 (RS) Ch1, 7dc into loop.
Round 2 2dc in first st, dc in each rem st around. [8 sts]
Round 3 Dc in each st around.
Pull the starting tail through the centre of the magic loop and out of the bottom of the Hand so that it can to be used later.

Rounds 4-5 Repeat Rounds 2-3. [9 sts]
Round 6 Ch2 (leaving a space for the Thumb to be sewn later), dc in each st of the Hand around. [11 sts]
Round 7 Dc in each st around, don't fasten off.
Sew the Thumb onto the Hand in the ch-2 sp of Round 6, taking the ends inside the Hand.
Take two pipe cleaners and twist them together. See Arm diagram on page 123. Fold this length in half, slip

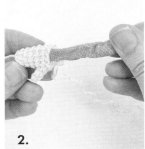
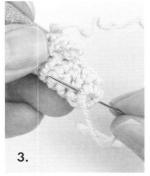

a paperclip over the loop that forms at the fold and twist the two ends of pipe cleaners together. Squeeze the paperclip so that it's as narrow as possible and put a bit of fabric dressing tape around the paperclip so that the ends of the wire are protected **{1}**. Put the paperclip end inside the Hand **{2}**. Use the starting tail of yarn to sew through the Hand and paperclip piece with a couple of small stitches **{3}**. Continue working around the pipe cleaner as follows **{4}**:
Round 8 Dec, dc in each rem st around. [10 sts]
Round 9 (Dec, 1dc) 3 times, 1dc. [7 sts]

Round 10 Dc in each st around.
Round 11 2dc in first st, dc in each rem st around. [8 sts]
Rounds 12-14 Dc in each st around.
Rounds 15-18 Repeat Rounds 11-14. [9 sts]
Round 19 2dc in first st, dc in each rem st around. [10 sts]
Rounds 20-26 Dc in each st around.
Decide whether the Arm will be right or left, and dc in each st to the underside of the arm, ss in next st, fasten off.

BODY

If you don't want to make removable underwear, work the Hip to Waist section in Soft Rose (10g) to take the place of pants. Finish the last round at the centre back and ss in the next st to make a neater join between the colours. You can neaten the joins afterwards by working a round of slip stitch surface crochet in Soft Rose following the join at the waist and legs.

Hip to Waist

See Hip to Waist Chart on page 122 for the starting Rows/Foundation Round of this section. This Chart also shows where the Leg sts will be sewn; these will be joined later.
With Nude and a 2.5mm hook ch9.
Row 1 (WS) Dc in second ch from hook and in each ch to end, turn. [8 sts]
Row 2 Ch1, dc in each st to end, rotate to work in row ends of the piece (gusset) just made.
Row 3 Ch1, 2dc in each row end, turn. [4 sts]
Row 4 Ch1, 2dc in first st, 2dc, 2dc in last st, turn. [6 sts]
Foundation Round (RS) Ch1, 2dc in first st, 4dc, 2dc in last st, ch42, ss in first st of round without twisting. [50 sts]
The first 8 sts form the centre front. The row ends of the gusset at the back will be sewn to the centre back 2

sts of the Foundation Round once the Leg and central wires have been joined.
Continue working in a spiral in front loops only.
Round 1 Dc in each st and ch around. [50 sts]
Rounds 2-6 Dc in each st around, don't fasten off.

Mark out the central front 10 sts. The first of these 10 sts will be the new start of the round. You might need to undo a stitch or two of the previous round to start the new round in this position.

Round 7 10dc, (dec, 6dc) 5 times. [45 sts]
Round 8 10dc, (dec, 5dc) 5 times. [40 sts]
Round 9 10dc, (dec, 4dc) 5 times. [35 sts]
Round 10 10dc, (dec, 3dc) 5 times. [30 sts]
Round 11 10dc, (dec, 2dc) 5 times, do not fasten off. [25 sts]

Waist to Underarms

Dc in each st around to centre back to re-position the start of the round.
Round 12 Dc in each st around.
Round 13 2dc, 2dc in next st, 7dc, 2dc in next st, 4dc, 2dc in next st, 7dc, 2dc in next st, dc in last st. [29 sts]
Round 14 3dc, 2dc in next st, 7dc, 2dc in next st, 6dc, 2dc in next st, 7dc, 2dc in next st, 2dc. [33 sts]
Round 15 4dc, 2dc in next st, 7dc, 2dc in next st, 8dc, 2dc in next st, 7dc, 2dc in next st, 2dc. [37 sts]
Round 16 Dc in each st around.
Round 17 5dc, 2dc in next st, 8dc, 2dc in next st, 9dc, 2dc in next st, 8dc, 2dc in next st, 3dc. [41 sts]
Round 18 Dc in each st around.
Mark out the central front 16 sts so that these can be worked in the back loops only on the following round. The yarn will be rejoined into these remaining loops later to work the Bust, which is worked in a separate piece, stuffed and sewn to the front of the Body.
Round 19 5dc, 2dc in next st, 30dc, working in

back loops only of central 16 sts, 2dc in next st, 4dc. [43 sts]

Round 20 6dc, 2dc in next st, 34dc, 2dc in next st, 1dc. [45 sts]

Round 21 Dc in each st around.

Round 22 7dc, 2dc in next st, 35dc, 2dc in next st, 1dc. [47 sts]

Round 23 Dc in each st around, do not fasten off.

BUST

It's easier to work the Bust at this point, before stuffing the Body. Join the beginning of a second ball of Nude or work in Soft Rose (5g) if you are making the Bra part of the doll. See Bust Chart on page 122. With Nude (or Soft Rose) and a 2.5mm hook join into the first remaining loop of central 16 sts from Round 18 with a dc. Leave a long starting tail for sewing the Bust to the Body once the Body and Bust have been stuffed.

Betty's Bust is worked separately

Row 1 (RS) Dc in next 2 sts, 1htr, 2tr in next st, 1htr, 4dc, 1htr, 2tr in next st, 1htr, 3dc, turn. [18 sts]

Row 2 Ch1, *2dc, 2htr, 1tr, 2tr in next st, 2htr, 2dc; rep from *, turn. [20 sts]

Row 3 Skip first st, *ss in next st, 1dc, 2htr, 2htr in next st, 2htr, 1dc, 1ss; rep from *, ss in next st, turn. [21 sts]

Row 4 Skip first ss, dc in next st, 3htr, 2htr in next st, 2htr, 1dc, 4ss, 1dc, 2htr, 2htr in next st, 3htr, 1dc, ss

in last unworked st from Row 2, turn. [23 sts]

Row 5 Skip ss, dc in next st, 1htr, 1tr, (tr2tog) twice, 1htr, 1dc, 1ss, skip 2 sts, ss in next st, 1dc, 1htr, (tr2tog) twice, 1tr, 1htr, 1dc, ss in last ss from Row 3, fasten off.

JOINING IN ARMS

When you align the arms, make sure the thumb is facing forward and the end of the final arm round is on the inside. Mark out the central front 16 sts in line with the Bust.

Round 24 Dc to 7 sts before central 16 sts, dec, 1dc, 7dc across top outside edge of arm, skip next 3 sts on Body, 1dc on Body, dc in central 16 sts, 1dc, 7dc across top outside edge of other arm, skip 3 sts on Body, 1dc, dec, dc in each rem st to end of round. [53 working sts]
Remove markers.

Round 25 Dc in each st up to Arm, dc in 7 Arm sts, dc in next st, dec, dc in each st to 3 sts before next Arm, dec, dc in next st, dc in 7 Arm sts and in each st to end. [51 sts]

Round 26 Dc in each st to 2 sts before first Arm, dec, dc in 7 sts of Arm and in each st to second Arm, dc in 7 sts of Arm, dec, dc in each st to end. [49 sts]

Round 27 3dc, (2dc, dec) twice, dc to last 11 sts, (dec, 2dc) twice, 3dc. [45 sts]

Round 28 6dc, dec, 7dc, dec, 11dc, dec, 7dc, dec, 6dc, do not fasten off. [41 sts]

JOINING LEGS

See Joining Legs Diagram on page 122.
The top of the two Leg wires are joined into the bottom of a central wire. The Leg wires are joined to the central wire with an extra short piece of wire {1} (you could use a straightened paperclip), passed through the loops of all three main pieces and wrapped round to secure {2}. The join should sit half way between the top of the Legs and where the waist will be when you've sewn the Legs to the Body, so

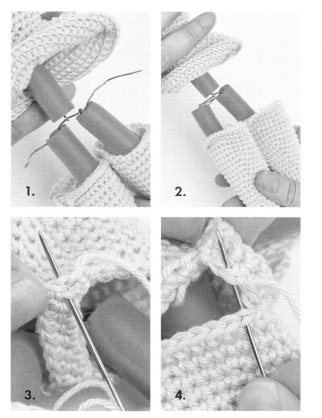

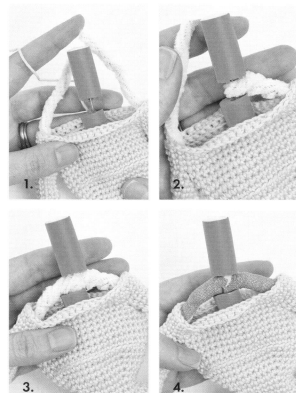

adjust the length of the Leg wires if necessary. Make sure you've got the Legs the right way round! Wrap a piece of fabric dressing tape around to cover the ends of wire.

With the Bust and the Feet facing forward, sew the back of the gusset to the central 2 back sts of the Foundation Round of the Body piece, with the central wire up through the centre of the Body, and the gusset between the two Leg wires {3}. See Hip to Waist Chart on page 122. Sew each Leg to the top of the Foundation Round, aligning the first ss at the front of each Leg with each outside dc st at the front of the Foundation Round {4}. The stitches of the Leg are matched to the stitches of the Foundation Round/gusset as shown on the Chart.

Stuff the Body up to the underarms.

WIRE IN ARMS

At the shoulders, you need to wrap the other end of the Arm pipe cleaners around the central wire. If using foam curlers, cut a section of the foam away using a craft knife to leave space to bend the pipe cleaners around {1}. The join should be no higher than the top of the crochet at this point. Bend the pipe cleaners around the central wire, making sure that the Arm can still fall straight to the side of the Body {2 and 3}. Twist the overlapped ends back around the Arm section of pipe cleaner to secure, and wrap a little fabric dressing tape around to protect the ends of the wire {4}. Use the tail of yarn at the underarm to sew up the gap. Repeat for the other Arm. Stuff the Body up to this point and top up the stuffing in the following rounds.

Round 29 5dc, dec, 6dc, dec, 11dc, dec, 6dc, dec,

5dc. [37 sts]

The following round uses dc2tog as the decrease method as there are quite a few decreases and the fabric needs additional structure.

Round 30 1dc, (1dc, dc2tog, 2dc, dc2tog) 5 times, 1dc. [27 sts]

Round 31 2dc, (dec, 2dc) 6 times, 1dc. [21 sts]

Round 32 2dc, (dec, 1dc) 6 times, 1dc. [15 sts]

Round 33 (Dec, 3dc) 3 times. [12 sts]

Rounds 34-35 Dc in each st around.

Dc in each st around to centre back, ss in next st, fasten off leaving a long tail.

Stuff the Bust and sew to the Body using the starting tail.

HEAD

This is the only piece of Betty that's worked from top down because it's easier to add the stuffing through the hole for the neck. The start of the round is at the centre back of the Head.

With Nude and a 2.5mm hook, make a magic loop.

Round 1 (RS) Ch1, 6dc into loop. [6 sts]

Work in a spiral in front loops only throughout.

Round 2 2dc in each st around. [12 sts]

Round 3 (2dc in next st, 1dc) 6 times. [18 sts]

Round 4 (2dc in next st, 2dc) 6 times. [24 sts]

Round 5 (2dc in next st, 3dc) 6 times. [30 sts]

Round 6 (2dc in next st, 4dc) 6 times. [36 sts]

Round 7 (2dc in next st, 5dc) 6 times. [42 sts]

Rounds 8-11 Dc in each st around.

Rounds 12-15 Dec, dc in each rem st around. [38 sts after Round 15]

Round 16 Dec, dc in each st to last 8 sts, (dec, 2dc) twice. [35 sts]

Round 17 (Dec, 2dc) twice, dc in each st to last 6 sts, (dec, 1dc) twice. [31 sts]

Round 18 (Dec, 1dc) twice, dc in each rem st around. [29 sts]

Round 19 2dc, (dec, 2dc) 6 times, 3dc. [23 sts]

Round 20 3dc, (dec, 1dc) 6 times, 2dc. [17 sts]

Round 21 2dc, (dec, 1dc) 5 times. [12 sts]

Ss in next st, fasten off and weave in ends.

Stuff the Head, leaving a space in the centre to insert the wire from the Body.

Face Details

Take a strand of black embroidery thread double the length you'll need (about 50cm). Fold this length in half and thread the needle over the two raw ends. When you make your first stitch, pass the needle through the loop at the fold. This means that you can avoid having to anchor the thread at the beginning. Sew the face details over the centre front stitches between Rounds 8 and 17, using the image and the Face Diagram on page 122 as a guide. Fasten off on the inside.

EARS (MAKE 2)

With Nude and a 2.5mm hook, ch3, 2tr in first of those ch, fasten off leaving a long tail. Unpick the beginning slip knot to make a neater finish. Align the top of the Ear with the top of Round 11, level with the top of the eyes, and leave 6 sts on each side between

the eyes and the Ear. Sew the Ears to the Head, rotating one ear to make a mirror image of the first. Sew a pearl bead to the bottom of each Ear as an earring.

Use the tail of yarn from the Body to sew the Head to the Body, topping up the stuffing as you go.

Weave in ends.

TO FINISH

If you've made the underwear part of the doll, you may wish to finish them by adding a small ribbon bow to the front of each, and ribbon ties on the Bra, as explained in the Bra and Pants patterns below.

HAIR IN A BUN

Materials

- Scheepjes Catona, Chocolate (15g)
- A 3mm hook
- Toy filling
- Black shirring elastic and hook and loop fastening if you want to make the hair removable (see note below)

Abbreviations

Ch-3 picot Ch3, ss in first of those ch

BEFORE YOU BEGIN

Removable Hair

Betty is designed to have removable hair so that she can change it to suit her mood. This is held in position by a piece of hook and loop fastening sewn onto the top of Betty's head, and inside the top of each hair

piece. If you prefer you can sew it to the Head, as this is an easier option. This hairstyle is a good one to choose if you want to sew it in place, as it goes with many outfits. It's not suited to having hats on top, so bear this in mind if you want to make the Head Scarf on page 63 or the Hat on page 117.

Construction

The Hair is made of three pieces and a Bun. The Right and Left Front pieces are sewn together, and edged around. They overlap the Back piece. The Bun is made separately, stuffed and sewn on top.

See Hair in a Bun Chart on page 123. Keep the ss fairly loose throughout. If it's difficult to get the hook into the last ss of the row, use a smaller hook for that stitch only.

RIGHT FRONT

With Chocolate and a 3mm hook, ch17.

Work in back loops only throughout.

Row 1 (RS) Ss in second ch from hook and next 3 ch, dc in next 8 ch, ss in last 4 ch, turn. [16 sts]

Rows 2-3 Ch1, 4ss, 8dc, 4ss, turn.

Rows 4-6 Ch1, 2ss, 12dc, 2ss, turn.

Rows 7-9 Ch1, 4ss, 8dc, 4ss, turn.

Row 10 Ch1, skip first st, 4ss, 6dc, 4ss, turn leaving last st unworked. [14 sts]

Row 11 Ch1, skip first st, 4ss, 4dc, 4ss, turn leaving last st unworked. [12 sts]

Row 12 Ch1, skip first st, 4ss, 2dc, 4ss, fasten off leaving a long tail and last st unworked.

LEFT FRONT

With Chocolate and a 3mm hook, ch6.

Work in back loops only throughout.

Row 1 (RS) Ch1, 2ss, 4dc, turn. [6 sts]

Row 2 Ch1, 4dc, 2ss, turn.

Row 3 Ch1, 2ss, dc in each st to last st, 2dc in last st, turn. [7 sts]

Row 4 Ch1, dc in each dc and ss in each ss from

previous row, turn.

Rows 5-6 Repeat Rows 3-4. [8 sts]

Row 7 Repeat Row 3, do not fasten off. [9 sts]
Rotate work and ss in each row end along the edge with the increase sts, fasten off leaving a long tail. Use the long tail on the Right Front to run a gathering thread down the right side so that this matches the length of the left side of the Left Front. Use the long tail from the Right Front to sew the two front pieces together. See the Hair in a Bun Chart on page 123.

Edging

Shown in green on the Hair in a Bun Chart.
Work in back loops only when working into the last row of Right and Left Fronts.
Rejoin Chocolate with a 3mm hook and RS facing in the last st of the Right Front.

Round 1 (RS) Ch2 (counts as htr), htr in each st of Row 12 to last st, (htr, ch1, htr) in last st, rotate to work in row ends, skip first row end, htr in next 10 row ends, ch-3 picot in corner, working in other side of foundation ch; (ss in next st, skip next st) 3 times, ss in next st, 4dc, 5ss, working in foundation ch of Left Front; ss in each st of foundation ch, ch-3 picot, rotate piece and work 5ss evenly in row ends to next corner, ss in each st of last row of Left Front, dc in end of seam between pieces, dc in base of beg ch-2, fasten off leaving a long tail.
Each ch-3 picot forms the piece in front of the ear.

BACK

With Chocolate and a 3mm hook, ch9.
Work in back loops only throughout.

Row 1 (RS) Htr in second ch from hook, htr in next ch, 4dc, 2ss, turn. [8 sts]

Row 2 Ch1, 2ss, 4dc, 2htr, turn.

Row 3 Ch1, 2htr, 4dc, 2ss, turn.

Rows 4-9 Repeat Rows 2-3.

Row 10 Ch1, 2ss, 4dc, 2htr, turn.

Row 11 Ch1, 2htr in first st, htr in next st, 4dc, 2ss, turn. [9 sts]

Row 12 Ch1, 2ss, 5dc, 2htr, turn.

Row 13 Ch1, 2htr in first st, htr in next st, 5dc, 2ss, turn. [10 sts]

Row 14 Ch1, 2ss, 6dc, 2htr, turn.

Row 15 Ch1, 2htr in first st, htr in next st, 6dc, 2ss, turn. [11 sts]

Row 16 Ch1, 2ss, 7dc, 2htr, turn.
Row 16 forms the centre back. From now on, the rows are a mirror image of the previous rows.

Row 17 Ch1, htr2tog, htr in next st, 6dc, 2ss, turn. [10 sts]

Row 18 As Row 14.

Row 19 Ch1, htr2tog, htr in next st, 5dc, 2ss, turn. [9 sts]

Row 20 As Row 12.

Row 21 Ch1, htr2tog, htr in next st, 4dc, 2ss, turn. [8 sts]

Row 22 As Row 10.

Rows 23-34 Repeat Row 3 for every RS row and Row 2 for every WS row.

Fasten off leaving a long tail and sew the sts of the last row to the sts of the foundation ch so that the piece forms a tube.

BUN

With Chocolate and a 3mm hook, ch13.
Work in back loops only throughout.

Row 1 Ss in second ch from hook, ss in next ch, 3dc, 2htr, 3dc, 2ss, turn. [12 sts]

Rows 2-30 Ch1, 2ss, 3dc, 2htr, 3dc, 2ss, turn.
Fasten off leaving a long tail. Sew the first row to the last row to make a tube. To gather the centre of the Bun, use the tail as a gathering thread along the row ends on one side, draw together and sew closed. Run another gathering thread along the outside edges of the Bun, pull up to close slightly and stuff but leave unsecured for the moment.

TO MAKE UP

Position the Back piece on the back of the Head with the centre Back aligned, pinning in place on the Head. With the ss edge of the Back piece in the centre, pinch the ss end of Rows 8-10 and Rows 22-24 together and pin so that there's a straight line of the row ends in between and sew into position {1}. Put the Bun on top, adjust the gathering thread and stuffing if necessary and sew to the Back piece around the back of the Bun {2}. Pin the Front pieces around the front of the Head, with the htr row of the Right Front piece coming up over the front of the Bun

slightly {3}. Sew these pieces together, being careful not to sew into the Head if you want to make the Hair removable {4}. Sew the Hair to the Head if you don't want interchangeable hairstyles.

If you want to make the Hair removable, run a doubled length of black shirring elastic along the inside around the edge, and pull it up slightly so that the elastic is under tension, secure the ends. Sew a piece of hook and loop fastening on the top of the Betty's Head and the inside of the Hair piece so that it will hold the Hair in position.

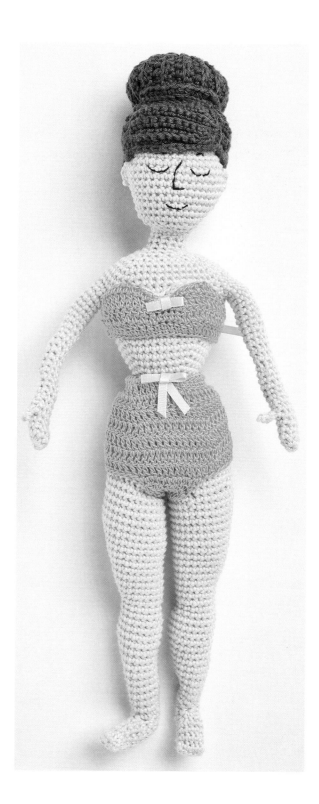

BRA
Materials
- Scheepjes Maxi Sweet Treat, Soft Rose (2g)
- A 2.5mm hook
- 50cm ribbon, 4mm wide
- Sewing thread
- Craft glue

Note
Made from the bottom up in rows with ribbon ties. A row of dc is worked into the other side of the foundation ch and the ties are sewn on afterwards.

With Maxi Soft Rose and a 2.5mm hook, ch29.
See Bra Chart on page 123.
Row 1 (RS) Dc in second ch from hook and next ch, 2htr, 5tr, 2tr in next ch, 2tr, 4htr, 2tr, 2tr in next ch, 5tr, 2htr, 2dc, turn. [30 sts]
Row 2 Ch1, 2dc, 2htr, 5tr, 2tr in next st, 3tr, 4htr, 3tr, 2tr in next st, 5tr, 2htr, 2dc, turn. [32 sts]
Row 3 Ch1, skip first st, ss in next st, 2dc, 2htr, 3tr, 2tr in next st, 2tr, 2htr, 4dc, 2htr, 2tr, 2tr in next st, 3tr, 2htr, 2dc, ss in next st, turn leaving last st unworked. [32 sts including ss]
Row 4 Skip ss, ss in next st, 2dc, 2htr, 2tr, tr2tog, tr in next st, 2htr, dc2tog, 2ss, dc2tog, 2htr, tr in next st, tr2tog, 2tr, 2htr, 2dc, ss in next st, fasten off. [26 sts including ss]

Rejoin Soft Rose in the other side of the foundation ch with a dc, dc in each st to end, fasten off and weave in ends.

TO FINISH
Cut two ribbon ties, each about 17cm long, and sew to the row ends on each side. Seal the raw ends with a little craft glue.

Make a small bow with a piece of ribbon 5cm long. Fold the ends into the centre back and take another small piece to wrap around the centre. Sew and/or stick it in position and sew to the centre of the Bra.

PANTS

Materials

▪ Scheepjes Maxi Sweet Treat, Soft Rose (5g)

▪ A 2.5mm hook

▪ 10cm ribbon, 4mm wide

▪ 30cm pink cord elastic

▪ Sewing thread

▪ Craft glue

Note

Made from the top down, back and forth in rows. The yarn is rejoined to work the gusset section from the bottom, the centre back seam is sewn part way and the back of the gusset is sewn to the centre back. The yarn is rejoined to work 2 rows into the foundation ch; the second of these rows is worked around the cord elastic to make a casing which is folded and sewn to the inside top of the Pants. A ribbon bow is sewn in place.

With Maxi Soft Rose and a 2.5mm hook, ch38.
Row 1 (RS) Tr in fourth ch from hook (skipped ch count as tr), tr in next 3 ch, 2tr in next ch, (8tr, 2tr in next ch) 3 times, 4tr, turn. [40 sts]
Row 2 Ch3 (counts as tr throughout), 4tr, 2tr in next st, 9tr, 2tr in next st, 8tr, 2tr in next st, 9tr, 2tr in next st, 5tr, turn. [44 sts]
Row 3 Ch3, 4tr, 2tr in next st, 10tr, 2tr in next st, 9tr, 2tr in next st, 10tr, 2tr in next st, 6tr, turn. [48 sts]
Row 4 Ch3, 5tr, 2tr in next st, 11tr, 2tr in next st, 10tr, 2tr in next st, 11tr, 2tr in next st, 6tr, turn. [52 sts]
Rows 5-6 Ch3, tr in each st to end, turn.
Fasten off.

Gusset

Skip the first 20 sts and rejoin Soft Rose in the next st with a ss.
Row 7 Ch2, tr in next st (counts as tr2tog throughout), 4tr, (tr2tog) twice, turn leaving rem sts unworked. [8 sts]
Row 8 Ch2, tr in next st, 4tr, tr2tog, turn. [6 sts]
Row 9 Ch2, tr in next st, (tr2tog) twice, turn. [3 sts]

Row 10 Ch3 (counts as tr throughout), tr in same st, (2tr in next st) twice, turn. [6 sts]
Row 11 Ch3, tr in same st, 4tr, 2tr in last st, turn. [8 sts]
Row 12 Ch3, tr in same st, 2tr in next st, 4tr, (2tr in next st) twice, fasten off leaving a long tail. [12 sts]

Sew the row ends of Rows 5 and 6 together to form the centre back seam, leaving the rest of the centre back open. Using the finishing tail, sew the 12 sts of the gusset to the centre back 12 sts.

Rejoin Soft Rose in the other side of the foundation ch with RS facing.
Row 1 (RS) Ch1, dc in each st to end, turn. [36 sts]
Row 2 Working in front loops only, and working each st around the cord elastic, ch1, dc in each st to end, fasten off leaving a long tail.

Tying off elastic

To hide the knot in the elastic, re-position the ends of the elastic as follows: Thread one of the ends of elastic onto a yarn needle and pass it through a few stitches on the WS on the opposite side of the gap, bringing it out on the WS. Pull out the other end of elastic so that it emerges at the same point. Tie a knot in the elastic so that the gap closes when the elastic is relaxed. Check at this point that the elastic will stretch far enough to fit over the Body, then thread each end of the elastic back through a few stitches and trim, sealing the ends of the elastic with a little craft glue.

Using the finishing tail, sew this final round to the inside of the waistband so that the elastic is hidden. Weave in ends.

Make a ribbon bow as for the Bra, adding longer ribbon tails if you wish. Seal the raw ends with craft glue and sew to the front of the Pants.

chapter three: betty at home

How does she do it? Betty always manages to look so glamorous, even in her pinny. Her Bakewell tarts are a thing of legend, don't you know. Bert wants a share, too, with his bowl at the ready. He's more likely to come running for a nice bit of salmon than the smell of freshly baked tarts though. Make sure he doesn't get confused for the neighbourhood Tomcat by giving him his own collar and name tag

Total yarn quantities for this section:
Scheepjes Catona 65g of Candy Apple (516), 30g of Jet Black (110), 35g of Snow White (106), 25g of Cyan (397), 30cm length of Apple Granny (513), 30cm length of Soft Rose (409).
Check the yarn quantities needed for all projects on page 121.

betty's red outfit

One wonders whether Betty's red dress is the most practical thing to be wearing for doing the housework, but she needs to keep up appearances at all times! The Peter Pan collar and flared skirt are the height of fashion

Materials
- Scheepjes Catona, Candy Apple (60g) Snow White (10g)
- A 2.5mm hook
- A 3mm hook
- 6 buttons, 5mm
- Sewing thread

See note about decreasing on page 10.

Note
The Skirt is worked first from the waist down in rows, leaving an opening at the centre back. The Sleeves are worked separately then the Body is worked onto the Skirt from the waist up to the armholes. The Sleeves are joined into the Body and worked as one piece to the neckline. Collar, Cuffs and Hem Trim are added afterwards. The bottom portion of the centre back seam is sewn and buttons and button loops are added to the centre back opening.

BETTY'S DRESS

Front

Back

SKIRT

With Candy Apple and a 3mm hook, ch26.

Row 1 (RS) Dc in second ch from hook and in each ch to end, turn. [25 sts]

Change to a 2.5mm hook.

Row 2 Ch3 (counts as tr throughout), tr in same st, 2tr in each st to end, turn. [50 sts]

Row 3 Ch3, 2tr in next st, (tr in next st, 2tr in next st) to end, turn. [75 sts]

Rows 4-6 Ch3, tr in each st to end, turn.

Change to a 3mm hook.

Row 7 Ch3, tr in each st to end, turn.

Row 8 Ch3, tr in next st, 2tr in next st, (2tr, 2tr in next st) to end, turn. [100 sts]

Rows 9-14 Ch3, tr in each st to end, turn.

Row 15 Ch1, dc in each st to end, fasten off leaving a long tail. Use the tail of yarn to sew the centre back seam up to Row 7. Leave the rest open to allow room to get the Dress on over Betty's hips.

SLEEVES (MAKE 2)

With Candy Apple and a 3mm hook, ch11 leaving a long starting tail.

Row 1 (RS) Dc in second ch from hook and in each ch to end, turn. [10 sts]

Rows 2-3 Ch1, dc in each st to end, turn.

Row 4 Ch1, 2dc in first st, dc in each st to end, turn. [11 sts]

Rows 5-7 Ch1, dc in each st to end, turn.

Row 8 Ch1, dc in each st to last st, 2dc in last st, turn. [12 sts]

Rows 9-11 Ch1, dc in each st to end, turn.

Row 12 As Row 4. [13 sts]

Rows 13-16 Repeat Rows 5-8. [14 sts after Row 8] Fasten off leaving a long tail. Use the starting tail to sew the Sleeve into a tube along the row ends.

BODY

With Candy Apple and a 3mm hook rejoin to the first st on the other side of the foundation ch of the Skirt with a dc.

Row 1 (RS) Dc in each rem st of foundation ch to end, turn. [25 sts]

Row 2 Ch1, 4dc, 2dc in next st, 3dc, 2dc in next st, 7dc, 2dc in next st, 3dc, 2dc in next st, 4dc, turn. [29 sts]

Row 3 Ch1, (4dc, 2dc in next st) twice, 9dc, (2dc in next st, 4dc) twice, turn. [33 sts]

Row 4 Ch1, (5dc, 2dc in next st) twice, 9dc, (2dc in next st, 5dc) twice, turn. [37 sts]

Row 5 Ch1, 6dc, 2dc in next st, 5dc, 2dc in next st, 11dc, 2dc in next st, 5dc, 2dc in next st, 6dc, turn. [41 sts]

Row 6 Ch1, 10dc, 2dc in next st, 19dc, 2dc in next st, 10dc, turn. [43 sts]

Rows 7-10 Ch1, dc in each st to end, turn.

Joining in Sleeves

Row 11 Ch1, 8dc, *holding Sleeve with seam underneath, dc in 9 uppermost sts of Sleeve, skip next 5 sts on Body**, dc in next 17 sts on Body; repeat from * to ** with other Sleeve, dc in last 8 sts on Body, turn. [51 working sts]

Row 12 Ch1, (7dc, dec) twice, 15dc, (dec, 7dc) twice, turn. [47 sts]

Row 13 Ch1, (6dc, dec) twice, 15dc, (dec, 6dc) twice, turn. [43 sts]

Row 14 Ch1, 6dc, dec, 4dc, dec, 15dc, dec, 4dc, dec, 6dc, turn. [39 sts]

Row 15 Ch1, 6dc, dec, 3dc, dec, 13dc, dec, 3dc, dec, 6dc, turn. [35 sts]

Row 16 Ch1, 5dc, dec, 3dc, dec, 11dc, dec, 3dc, dec, 5dc, turn. [31 sts]

Row 17 Ch1, 4dc, dec, 3dc, dec, 9dc, dec, 3dc, dec, 4dc, turn, do not fasten off. [27 sts]

Shaping at Neckline

Row 18 Ch1, skip st at base of ch, 2ss, *dc in next st, htr in next st, tr in next st, tr2tog, tr in next st, htr in next st, dc in next st, 6ss; rep from * once more

omitting last 4 ss, fasten off. [24 sts]
Weave in ends, and sew up gap at each underarm using the tail from the Sleeves.

Buttonholes

Rejoin Candy Apple with RS facing at the top of the centre back seam of the Skirt on the left edge. Dc evenly along row ends of the Skirt with the last dc in the end of Row 1 of the Body. (Ch1, skip next row end, dc in next 2 row ends) 5 times, skip next row end, dc in last row end, fasten off and weave in ends. Sew six buttons to right back edge to match the ch-1 buttonhole spaces.

CUFFS

Worked back and forth in rows, leaving a gap on the underside so that you can get the Hand through the Sleeve.
Join Snow White to the end of the Sleeve by the Sleeve seam with RS facing and a 2.5mm hook.
Row 1 (RS) Working in the other side of the foundation ch, ch1, dc in each st to end, turn. [10 sts]
Row 2 Ch1, dc in each st to end, turn.
Row 3 Ch1, dc2tog, dc in each st to last 2 sts, dc2tog, fasten off and weave in ends.
Repeat for the other Cuff.

COLLAR
Right Collar Piece
With Snow White and a 2.5mm hook, ch15.
Row 1 (RS) Dc in second ch from hook, 2dc, (2dc in next st, dc in next st) 5 times, ss in last ch, turn. [19 sts]
Row 2 Ch1, dc2tog, dc in each st to end, turn. [18 sts]
Row 3 Ch1, 2dc, (2dc in next st, 5dc) twice, 2dc in next st, dc in next st, dc2tog, fasten off and weave in ends.

Left Collar Piece
With Snow White and a 2.5mm hook, ch15.
Row 1 (RS) Ss in second ch from hook, (dc in next st, 2dc in next st) 5 times, 3dc, turn. [19 sts]
Row 2 Ch1, dc in each st to last 2 sts, dc2tog, turn. [18 sts]
Row 3 Ch1, dc2tog, dc in next st, (2dc in next st, 5dc) twice, 2dc in next st, 2dc, fasten off and weave in ends.

The front ends of each Collar piece are the ends with the decreases. With the front ends of the Collar pieces meeting at the centre front of the neckline, sew in place with sewing thread. If the Collar doesn't lie flat, try blocking it with spray starch. You could also sew the points of the Collar to the Dress.

HEM TRIM
With Snow White and a 2.5mm hook, (ch13, ss in 7th ch from hook) repeat until trim is long enough to fit around hem edge, sew in place using sewing thread.

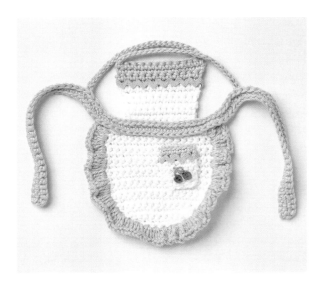

Row 14 Ch1, dc in each st to end, turn.
Rows 15-16 As Row 13. [11 sts after Row 16]
Row 17 Ch1, skip first st, dc2tog, dc in each st to last 3 sts, skip next st, dc2tog, turn. [7 sts]
Row 18 Ch1, skip first st, ss in next st, 3dc, ss in next st, fasten off leaving last st unworked.

Frill
Join Cyan to top left edge with RS facing and a 3mm hook. Work 3tr in each row end to last row, 3tr in each st of last row and 3tr in each row end up other side. Fasten off leaving a long tail. Use the tail of yarn to thread through the base of the stitches and pull up, so that the Frill gathers more easily.

BIB
With Snow White and a 3mm hook, join with a dc in the fourth st of the foundation ch on the Bottom piece of the Apron with RS facing.
Row 1 (RS) 10dc in the other side of the foundation ch, turn leaving rem sts unworked (leaving 3 sts unworked at the beginning and end of the row). [11 sts]
Rows 2-6 Ch1, dc in each st to end, turn.
Rows 7-8 Ch1, 2dc in first st, dc in each st to end, turn. [13 sts after Row 8]
Change to Cyan.
Rows 9-11 Ch1, dc in each st to end, turn.
Row 12 *Ch26, Ss in second ch from hook and in each ch back to Bib, ss in st at base of ch,** (first strap made) dc in each st to last st, ss in last st; rep from * to ** for second strap, fasten off and weave in ends.

POCKET
With Snow White and a 3mm hook, ch7.
Row 1 (RS) Dc in second ch from hook and in each ch to end, turn. [6 sts]
Rows 2-3 Ch1, dc in each st to end, turn.
Row 4 Ch1, dc2tog, 2dc, dc2tog, turn. [4 sts]
Row 5 Ch1, skip first st, 2dc, ss in last st, fasten off

APRON
Materials
■ Scheepjes Catona,
   Snow White (15g)
   Cyan (10g)
   A 30cm length of Apple Granny

■ A 3mm hook

■ 15cm of pink mini ricrac braid

■ 2 red buttons, 5mm

■ Craft glue

Note
The Bottom section of the Apron is made first top down, then the Bib and Strap section is worked bottom up from the foundation chain of the Bottom section. The Waist Tie is made separately and sewn to the join between the sections, then the Straps are crossed at the back, sewn to the Waist Tie and the Pocket is sewn to the front.

BOTTOM SECTION
With Snow White and a 3mm hook, ch18.
Row 1 (RS) Dc in second ch from hook and in each ch to end, turn. [17 sts]
Rows 2-12 Ch1, dc in each st to end, turn.
Row 13 Ch1, dc2tog, dc in each st to last 2 sts, dc2tog, turn. [15 sts]

The Apron ties cross over at the back

leaving a long tail.
Join Cyan with a dc in the first st on the other side of the foundation ch with WS facing.
Row 1 (WS) Dc in each rem st on the other side of the foundation ch, turn.
Row 2 Ch1, dc in each st to end, fasten off and weave in Cyan ends and the starting Snow White end.

Cut a piece of ricrac braid slightly wider than the Pocket, so that you can fold the ends to the WS on each side. Glue in position over the join between Cyan and Snow White. Split a strand of Apple Granny in half, and use one half to embroider a chain stitch leaf and two straight stitches for stems. Glue or sew the buttons on the end of the stalks.

WAIST TIE
With Cyan and a 3mm hook, ch81.
Dc in second ch from hook and in each ch to last ch, 4dc in last ch, rotate to work on other side of foundation ch, dc in each st to last st, 3dc in last st, ss to first dc, fasten off and weave in ends.

TO MAKE UP
Find the centre of the Waist Tie and align it with the

centre of the Bib/Bottom Section, to sew it across the join of the two sections. Put the Apron on Betty over the Dress, cross the Straps at the back and sew the end of each Strap to the Waist Tie, with enough space between the Straps in the centre to tie the Tie. You'll need to take the Apron off over Betty's head. Cut a piece of ricrac slightly wider than the Bib of the Apron so that you can fold each end to the WS. Place the ricrac over the join between Cyan and Snow White and stick in position. Split the ending tail of the Pocket in half and use one half to sew the Pocket to the Apron in one direction, and the other half of the tail in the other direction.

LOW-HEELED SHOES
Materials
■ Scheepjes Catona, Jet Black (5g)

■ A 2.5mm hook

■ 2 paperclips, 3cm long

■ Craft glue

■ Lining fabric for insoles (see note on page 11)

■ Wire cutters

Note
These heeled shoes use a paperclip to enable you to bend the Sole into position. You can use a piece of lining fabric as an insole to cover the paperclip if you wish. If you choose to do this, draw around the Sole on the lining fabric to use as a guide before you complete the shoe.

SOLE AND UPPER
See Low-Heeled Shoe Chart on page 125.

Sole
With Jet Black and a 2.5mm hook, ch11 leaving a long starting tail. Work in a spiral without closing off the end of the round.

Round 1 (RS) Htr in third ch from hook (counts as 2 htr), dc in next 5 ch, htr in next ch, tr in next ch, (tr, 4htr, tr) in next ch, rotate to work on other side of

34

foundation ch, tr in next ch, htr in next ch, dc in next 5 ch, (2htr, 4tr) in next ch, do not fasten off. [28 sts]

Upper
Round 2 Working in back loops only; dc in top of beg ch-2, dc2tog, 2dc, (dc2tog, 4dc) twice, dc2tog, 2dc, dc2tog, 5dc. [23 sts]
Round 3 7dc, htr in next st, htr3tog, htr in next st, 11dc. [21 sts]
Round 4 (partial round) 6dc, ch3 for strap, fasten off and weave in ends.

Heel piece
With Jet Black and a 2.5mm hook, ch3 leaving a long starting tail.
Row 1 2htr in third ch from hook, fasten off leaving a long tail.

TO MAKE UP
Follow the instructions for making up the Dancing Shoes on page 105. The Heel piece on these shoes is smaller than the other shoes; instead of rolling the Heel Piece as directed for the Dancing Shoes, just use the starting tail to sew the last htr to the beg ch-2 along the length of the post of the st. Trim the paperclip so that it is shorter than the heel length and put a blob of glue on the end of the heel to stop the wire of the clip poking through. Use the ending tail to sew the ch-3 strap to the opposite side of the Shoe once the paperclip and insole are in place.

HEADBAND
Materials
■ Scheepjes Catona, Candy Apple (5g)

■ A 3mm hook

Band
With Candy Apple and a 3mm hook, ch39.
Ss in second ch from hook and in each ch to end, fasten off and sew two ends together without twisting the band.

Bow
With Candy Apple and a 3mm hook, ch17.
Row 1 Dc in second ch from hook and in each ch to end, fasten off leaving a long tail. [16 sts]
Sew the first st to the last st to form a ring.

With Candy Apple, ch9, ss in second ch from hook and in each ch to end, fasten off leaving a long tail. Flatten the ring made from the dc row and put this ss piece around the centre, using the tail of yarn to sew the two ends together, then sew the bow to the join of the Band.

SITTING-UP BERT

Materials

■ Scheepjes Catona, Jet Black (25g)

■ A 30cm length of Scheepjes Catona, Soft Rose

■ 2 30cm lengths of Scheepjes Catona, Snow White

■ A 2.5mm hook

■ Black pipe cleaner, 30cm

■ Plastic toy filling granules

■ Old black tights

■ Craft glue

See note about decreasing on page 10.

Measurements

Bert measures 9cm tall.

Note

The Body is worked from the Neck down with an opening

so that the Front Leg piece can be worked from here later. The Front Leg piece is worked in one piece and then sewn down the centre to create the appearance of two legs. A pipe cleaner is used to reinforce the legs and neck, and a Base is worked separately and sewn on after the stuffing and granules for weighting are added. The Head and Ears are made separately and sewn onto the Neck.

Some of the step-by-step photos are shown using yellow yarn rather than black to make it easier to see the details.

BODY

With Jet Black and a 2.5mm hook, ch10 leaving a long starting tail, ss to first ch to join being careful not to twist. Work in a spiral in front loops only unless instructed otherwise.

Round 1 (RS) Ch1, dc in each ch around. [10 sts]

Rounds 2-3 Dc in each st around.

Round 4 2dc in first st, dc in each rem st around. [11 sts]

Round 5 As Round 4. [12 sts]

Round 6 (2dc in next st, dc in next st) 6 times. [18 sts]

Round 7 2dc in first st, dc in next st, 2dc in next st, dc in each st around to last 3 sts, 2dc in next st, dc in next st, 2dc in last st. [22 sts]

Round 8 (Dc in next st, 2dc in next st) twice, 4dc, ch6, skip next 6 sts, 4dc, (2dc in next st, dc in next st) twice. [20 dc, 6 ch]

In the following round you'll work into the sts of the previous round and the 6 chain sts, leaving an opening for joining the Front Leg piece later.

Round 9 2dc, 2dc in next st, dc in next st, 2dc in next st, 5dc, dc in each ch, 5dc, 2dc in next st, dc in next st, 2dc in next st, 2dc. [30 sts]

Rounds 10-11 Dc in each st around.

Round 12 Dc in first st, 2dc in next st, 3dc, 2dc in next st, dc in each st around to last 6 sts, 2dc in next st, 3dc, 2dc in next st, dc in last st. [34 sts]

Rounds 13-14 Dc in each st around.

Round 15 4dc, dec, dc in each st around to last 6 sts, dec, 4dc, do not fasten off. [32 sts]

TAIL AND BACK PAWS

The Tail and Back Paws are all worked onto stitches of the next round. The Tail is made by working part of the round and adding a few chain for the end of the tail, then working 2 more rows on these stitches. The original round is continued by working back and forth on a few stitches for each Back Paw, then the round is completed and extra stitches are worked across the back part of the round only before sewing the Tail and the Feet in place. See Tail and Back Paws Chart on page 125.

Tail

Working in front loops only as before:
Row 1 (RS) 10dc, ch5, turn.
Now working in back loops of each st:
Row 2 Dc in second ch from hook, in next 3 ch and in next 10 dc, ss in front loop of next unworked st of original round, turn. [14dc, 1ss]
Now working in both loops of each st for rest of Tail:
Row 3 Skip ss, 14dc, turn. [14 dc]
Row 4 Ch1, 14dc, ss in same st as previous ss, fasten off leaving long tail for sewing.

First Back Paw

Rejoin Jet Black with a 2.5mm hook in the next unworked st of the original round with a ss, leaving a long starting tail for sewing and working in front loops only:
Row 1 (RS) Beg in st after ss, 4dc, turn. [4 sts]
Working in both loops:
Row 2 Ch1, 3dc, ss in next st, turn. [3 sts and 1ss]
Row 3 Skip ss, 3dc, don't fasten off.

Working in front loops only, ss in base of same st at end of Row 1 and in next 3 unworked sts of the original round.

Second Back Paw

Working in front loops only:

Row 1 (RS) Ch1, dc in same st as last ss, dc in next 3 sts, ss in next st, turn. [4 sts and 1 ss]
Working in both loops only for rest of Paw:
Row 2 Skip ss, ss in next st, 3dc, turn. [4 sts]
Row 3 Ch1, 3dc, ss in next st, fasten off leaving a tail for sewing.

Extra Rows at Back

Rejoin Jet Black with a 2.5mm hook with a ss in the same st as the ss at the end of Row 1 of the Second Paw.
Row 1 (RS) Working in front loops only, dc in next st and in each rem st of round, dc in ss at fasten off point of Tail, then working underneath the tail, dc in the rem front loops from Row 1 of Tail of the next 11 sts to end of where Tail is joined to Body, ss in same st as last st of tail joined to Body, turn.
Row 2 (WS) Skip ss, dc in next 10 sts back to start of round, then continue in same direction with dc in next 10 sts, ss in next st, fasten off.

Bert's tail is joined to the Body part-way around the back

Finish Paws and Tail

The extra stitches for the Front Paws should naturally curl under slightly, but you can use the starting/ending tails to sew the two outside top stitches of each Paw to the underneath side to hold them in place. Curl the last row of the Tail towards the Body, and use the ending tail to sew it in place, making sure you leave the last round of Body stitches free for sewing to the Base. Sew to the end of the Tail, sewing the last row to the foundation ch at the end of the Tail.

FRONT LEG PIECE
With RS facing and the neck towards you, rejoin Jet Black with a 2.5mm hook at the right hand side of the opening for the Front Leg Piece.
Round 1 (RS) Working in front loops only throughout, dc in each of the opening sts, and add 1 extra st at each side of the opening. [14 sts]
Continue working in a spiral:
Round 2 Dc in each st around, skipping 1 st at what will be the back of the Leg Piece. [13 sts]
Rounds 3-6 As Round 2. [9 sts after Round 6]
Row 7 Ch1, 8dc, turn leaving last st unworked. [8 sts]
Row 8 Ch1, dc2tog, 4dc, dc2tog, fasten off leaving a long tail for sewing.
These last 2 rows will form the Paws and will be folded forward.

To Make up Front Legs
See Front Leg Piece Diagram on page 125. Fold pipe cleaner in half, then fold up the ends of the pipe cleaner so that they're doubled for about 5cm at each end (this is approx the length of the Front Leg Piece). Twist each of these doubled sections {1}. Insert the folded pipe cleaner twisted ends first, down the neck and down through the Front Leg Piece, until the ends reach the Paws {2}. Pinch the Paws section flat, and use the long finishing tail to sew up the end of the Piece, over the ends of the pipe cleaner. Work a long straight stitch in the centre of the Paws and pull tight to create an indent between the two Paws {3}. Continue working tight back stitches through both layers of the Front Leg Piece, in between the two pipe cleaners, to make the distinction between the two

front legs. Once you've worked a few back stitches through the Front Leg only, continue the back stitches, working also through the Body so that the Front Leg piece is secured to the Body {4}. Stop when you reach Round 2 of the Front Leg Piece and fasten off on the inside of the Body.

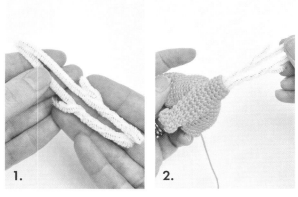

1.   2.

3.

4.

BASE

With Jet Black and a 2.5mm hook, make a magic loop.

Round 1 (RS) Ch1, 6dc into loop. [6 sts]
Round 2 2dc in each st around. [12 sts]
Round 3 (1dc, 2dc in next st) 6 times. [18 sts]
Round 4 (2dc, 2dc in next st) 6 times. [24 sts]
Round 5 (3dc, 2dc in next st) 6 times. [30 sts]
Round 6 (partial round) 4dc, 2dc in next st, 4dc, ss in next st, fasten off leaving a long tail for sewing to the Body.

Filling

Cut one toe from the tights about 10cm from the toe seam. Put plastic granules inside the toe until you get a ball about the size of a walnut. Twist the top and check the fit inside the Body, adding or removing granules if necessary. Sew the top securely, wrapping any overlap from the tights back around the ball. Place the ball inside the Body, and using the long tail, sew the Base to the Body, using the remaining loops of sts inside the Tail and the Paws, fasten off.

HEAD

Worked from side to side in front loops only.
With Jet Black and a 2.5mm hook, make a magic loop.

Round 1 (RS) Ch1, 6dc into loop. [6 sts]
Round 2 (1dc, 2dc in next st) 3 times. [9 sts]
Round 3 (2dc, 2dc in next st) 3 times. [12 sts]
Round 4 (3dc, 2dc in next st) 3 times. [15 sts]
Round 5 Dc in each st around.
Round 6 (4dc, 2dc in next st) 3 times. [18 sts]
Round 7 Ch3, skip 3 sts, dc in each rem st around (this creates an opening for the Neck).
Round 8 Working into sts and ch, (dec, 4dc) 3 times. [15 sts]
Round 9 Dc in each st around.
Round 10 (Dec, 3dc) 3 times. [12 sts]
Round 11 (Dec, 2dc) 3 times, fasten off leaving a tail

for sewing up. [9 sts]
There isn't a final round of 6 sts missing; the sewing up will take the place of this round otherwise the Head doesn't look symmetrical.
Run the finishing tail around the remaining sts, pull closed and secure, weave in ends.
Cut small pieces from the black tights and use these to stuff the Head.

EARS (MAKE 2)

With Jet Black and a 2.5mm hook, make a magic loop.
Work Rounds 1 and 2 as for Head, fasten off leaving a tail for sewing. Pinch flat and pull into a pointed shape. Sew on each side of the Head using the image as a guide.
Weave in all ends.

The finishing details for Bert's face and paws

FACE DETAILS

Take a length of Soft Rose and split it in half. Using one half, sew straight stitches on the inside of the Ears to make a triangular shape, using the image as a guide. Repeat for the Nose. Split a strand of Snow White and sew two 'V' shapes for the eyes, and the mouth using back stitches. Split a strand of Jet Black and sew through the cheeks on both sides to form whiskers. Trim the ends to length, and keeping the strands separate, put glue on each whisker to stiffen.

TO FINISH

Run the starting thread from the Neck around the top Neck stitches and pull tight. Push the Neck into the hole in the Head so that the first round of the Neck is inside the hole. You can use the blunt end of a crochet hook to do this. You'll probably need to fold the end of the doubled pipe cleaner over so that it isn't too long, but this will help reinforce the Neck. Sew the Head in place on the Neck. Using a split strand of Snow White, sew three straight stitches on each of the four paws.

BERT'S COLLAR
Materials
- Scheepjes Catona, Cyan (5g) Snow White (5g)
- A 30cm length of Scheepjes Catona, Jet Black
- A 2.5mm hook
- A 3mm hook
- Button, 5mm
- 1 large jump ring (jewellery supplier)
- 2 small jump rings (jewellery supplier)
- A small toy bell
- Lining fabric (see note on page 11)
- Craft glue
- Glue gun

With Cyan and a 3mm hook, ch13.
Row 1 Dc in second ch from hook and in each ch to end, ch4, ss in end of row to form a button loop, fasten off and weave in ends.

Sew the button on the opposite end of the Collar from the button loop.

NAME LABEL
With Snow White and a 2.5mm hook, ch4.
Row 1 Dc in second ch from hook and next 2 ch, turn. [3 sts]
Rows 2-3 Ch1, 3dc, turn.
Fasten off and weave in ends.

Split a length of Jet Black, and use to sew the letter B on the Label.

TO MAKE UP

If you wish you can stick a small piece of lining fabric on the reverse of the label to hide the sewing and seal in the ends. Attach a small jump ring to the top of the Label and to the bell, and put these small rings on the larger jump ring. Sew the large jump ring to the centre of the Collar. Use a small blob of glue gun glue applied with a cocktail stick to seal the joins in the jump rings.

BERT'S BOWL

■ Scheepjes Catona,
  Cyan (10g)
  Snow White (5g)

■ A 30cm length of Scheepjes Catona, Jet Black

■ A 2.5mm hook

■ A 3mm hook

■ Craft glue

TOP

With Cyan and a 3mm hook, make a magic loop.
Round 1 (RS) Ch1, 6dc into loop, ss to first dc to join. [6 sts]
Round 2 Ch1, 2dc in each st around, ss to first dc. [12 sts]
Round 3 Ch1, (1dc, 2dc in next st) 6 times, ss to first dc. [18 sts]
Round 4 Ch1, (2dc, 2dc in next st) 6 times, ss to first dc. [24 sts]
Round 5 Working in back loops only, ch1, dc in each st around, ss to first dc.
Round 6 Ch1, 2dc in first st, dc in each rem st around, ss to first dc. [25 sts]
Rounds 7-8 As Round 6. [27 sts after Round 8]
Fasten off.

BASE

With Cyan and a 3mm hook, make a magic loop. Work in a spiral without closing off each round with a ss.
Round 1 (RS) 6dc into loop. [6 sts]
Round 2 2dc in each st around. [12 sts]
Round 3 (1dc, 2dc in next st) 6 times. [18 sts]
Round 4 (2dc, 2dc in next st) 6 times. [24 sts]
Round 5 (3dc, 2dc in next st) 6 times, ss in next st, fasten off leaving a long tail. [30 sts]

Use the long tail to begin sewing the Base to the Top, using both top loops of the Base sts, but only the outside loop of the Top sts. Once you've got half way round, put some glue on the underside of the Top piece to stick it to the Base in the centre. Continue sewing all the way round. Fasten off and weave in ends.

Make a Name Label as for Bert's Collar leaving a long tail of yarn and use the tail to sew the Label to the front of the Bowl.

chapter four:
betty at the movies

'Breakfast at Betty's' may well be the next box office hit! Help Betty channel her inner Audrey Hepburn in her slim-fitting dress and stole with all the bling. For a dress worthy of the red carpet you can also make Betty's oh-so-elegant evening gown with stunning train detail. Bert looks the part too, having scooped his own award at the Cat Academy. Who knew such a thing existed?

Total yarn quantities for this section: Scheepjes Catona 45g of Delphinium (113), 15g of Jet Black (110), 5g of Chocolate (507), 80g of Lilac Mist (399), 1m length of Nude (255) **Scheepjes Panda** (100% polyester, 50g/90m) 20g of Husky (583). 5g of Gold lurex yarn, fingering weight. Check the yarn quantities needed for all projects on page 121.

betty's sheath dress

This figure-hugging number is made in a regal purple, worthy of a big screen star.
The rib stitch pattern and slip stitch panels at the waist keep the dress form-fitting.
The diamond-studded belt is made from a hair elastic and costume gems

Materials

- Scheepjes Catona, Delphinium (45g)
- A 3mm hook
- Hair elastic for belt (see note below)
- Acrylic rhinestones or costume jewellery
- Clip-on earring for brooch
- 2 press fasteners
- Glue gun
- Wire cutters

Note

The Sheath Dress is worked from side to side in rows from a (dc, ch1) rib, with slip stitch sections to shape the waist. The Shoulder Band is worked separately in the round and sewn on, leaving enough space for the armholes. The hair elastic used for the Belt should be big enough to fit over Betty's hips, and it's easier to use one that's made with thicker elastic. The one I used measured 8cm long when folded flat, with elastic 5cm wide.

In the (dc, ch1) rib pattern beg in Row 2, ch always count as sts and total st count remains constant for the Body section.

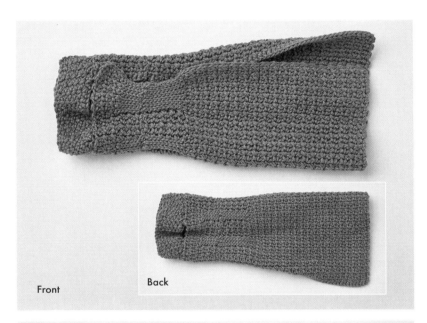

Front   Back

Dress laid flat

BODY

The Body of the dress overlaps at the front with a hidden fastening. This makes it easy to adjust the fit. With Delphinium and a 3mm hook, ch60.

Row 1 (RS) Dc in second ch from hook and in each ch to end, turn. [59 sts]

Row 2 Ch1, dc in first st, (ch1, skip next st, dc in next st) repeat to end, turn.

Rows 3-10 As Row 2.

Row 11 Ch1, dc in first dc, (ch1, skip next ch, dc in next dc) twice, ss in back loops only of next 17 sts, dc in next dc, (ch1, skip next ch, dc in next dc) repeat to end, turn.

Row 12 Ch1, dc in first dc, (ch1, skip next ch, dc in next dc) until you reach ss of previous row, ss in back loops only of next 17 sts, (ch1, skip next ch, dc in next dc) repeat to end, turn.

Rows 13-15 Repeat Rows 11-12, then Row 11 again.

Rows 16-20 Ch1, dc in first st, (ch1, skip next st, dc in next st) repeat to end, turn.

Repeat Rows (11-20) twice more.

Repeat Rows (11-12) 6 more times, and Row 11 once more, fasten off.

SHOULDER BAND

With Delphinium and a 3mm hook, ch59.

Row 1 (RS) Dc in second ch from hook and in each ch to end, do not turn, and work the first st of the next round in the first st of Row 1, being careful not to twist and joining into the round. Continue working in a spiral without closing off each round with ss. [58 sts]

Rounds 2-4 (Dc in next st, ch1, skip next st) repeat around.

Round 5 (Dc in next 3 dc skipping the ch-sps, ch1) repeat to last 4 sts, dc in last 2 dc skipping the ch-sps. [38 sts]

Round 6 (Dc in next dc, ch1, skip next st) around, ss in first st of next round to end, fasten off.

Sew the starting tail to the next st to even the join in the first round, fasten off and weave in ends.

Sew on press fasteners to keep the wrapover dress closed

TO MAKE UP

See Sheath Dress Shoulder Band Diagram on page 126. Wrap the Body around Betty so that the overlap sits at the Left Front and the second two slip stitch sections are centred at the back. Secure temporarily with a pin. Put the Shoulder Band over the shoulders with the narrow opening at the top, and position it so that the bottom edge just overlaps the top of the Body. With a piece of waste yarn, tack the top of the Body to the Shoulder Band from the front overlap edge for approx 4cm, working through the top layer only and leaving a gap before you reach the arm. Repeat across the centre back, leaving gaps for the arms. Take the Dress off over the head, and turn inside out, before sewing the Shoulder Band to the top of the Body with the WS facing, fasten off.

BELT

With Delphinium and a 3mm hook, work dc sts into the hair elastic loop so that they cover half of the elastic. I used a stretchy rhinestone bracelet to cover the front half of the Belt. Cut a section of the bracelet using wire cutters and remove the elastic from the bracelet. Stick each end of the bracelet to the hair elastic using a glue gun, and sew through the hair elastic and around the bracelet at intervals. Fasten off each time you sew so that the elastic can still stretch. Alternatively you could stick acrylic rhinestones to the front of the Belt, or for a simple fastening, use a piece of ribbon.

TO FINISH

Sew a press fastener to the top corner underneath the overlap, and under the overlap of the skirt, approx 6cm down from the waist.

For a brooch, I used a clip-on earring from a charity shop, changing the rhinestones to match the colour of the Dress. You could also use a brooch back or clip-on earring base from a jewellery supplier to make your own by sticking on acrylic rhinestones.

Block the skirt with water or spray starch to stop the hem curling.

STOLE
■ Scheepjes Panda, Husky (20g)

■ A 4.5mm hook

Note
It can be difficult to see the position of the stitches when working with this yarn, but as long as you count the stitches as you're working in each row, it seems to work out fine!

With Husky and a 4.5mm hook, ch10.
Row 1 Dc in second ch from hook and in each ch to end, turn. [9 sts]
Row 2 Ch1, dc in each st to end, turn.
Repeat Row 2 until piece measures 32cm, fasten off and weave in ends.

HIGH-HEELED EVENING SHOES
■ Scheepjes Catona, Jet Black (5g)

■ A 2.5mm hook

■ 2 paperclips, 3cm long

■ Acrylic rhinestones

■ Craft glue

Note
Each shoe is made with 2 Sole pieces which sandwich the paperclip as used for the Dancing Shoes method explained on page 105.

SOLE (make 2 per shoe)
With Jet Black and a 2.5mm hook, ch11 leaving a long starting tail on one of the Sole pieces on each shoe. Work in a spiral without closing off the end of the round.
Round 1 (RS) Htr in third ch from hook (counts as 2 htr), dc in next 5 ch, htr in next ch, tr in next ch, (tr, 4htr, tr) in next ch, rotate to work on other side of foundation ch, tr in next ch, htr in next ch, dc in next 5 ch, (2htr, 4tr) in next ch, ss to top of beg ch-2, fasten off leaving a long tail on one of the Sole pieces per shoe. [28 sts]

HEEL PIECE

With Jet Black and a 2.5mm hook, ch4 leaving a long starting tail.

Row 1 Dc in second ch from hook and in next 2 ch, turn. [3 sts]

Row 2 Ch2, htr in st at base of ch, (dc, ss) in next st, turn leaving last st unworked.

Row 3 Ch1, skip ss, dc in dc, htr in htr, turn. [2 sts]

Row 4 As Row 2.

Fasten off leaving a long tail.

FRONT BAND

With Jet Black and a 2.5mm hook, ch7 leaving a long starting tail.

Row 1 Dc in second ch from hook and in each ch to end, turn. [6 sts]

Row 2 Ch1, dc in each st to end, fasten off leaving a long tail.

TO MAKE UP

Follow the instructions for making up the Dancing Shoes on page 105, sewing the paperclip to the Sole piece with the long starting tail on each shoe. Once you have the paperclip and Heel Piece in position, sew the other Sole piece on top of the first to hide the paperclip, using the long ending tail. Sew the Front Band on the shoe using the starting and ending tails and stick rhinestones to the Band.

TIARA

■ Scheepjes Catona, Chocolate (5g)

■ A 3mm hook

■ Hair elastic (see note on Sheath Dress for size)

■ Costume jewellery, acrylic rhinestones or other decoration

■ Glue gun or craft glue

With Chocolate and a 3mm hook, work dc sts into the hair elastic loop so that they completely cover the

elastic, ss to first st, turn.

Row 1 (WS) 11dc, ss in next st, turn leaving rem sts unworked. [11 sts not including ss]

Row 2 Skip ss, dc2tog, 7dc, dc2tog, ss in next st, fasten off and weave in ends.

Stick or sew rhinestones, pieces of costume jewellery or other decoration to the front of the Tiara. Rhinestones will probably stick with craft glue, but you may need a glue gun for sticking metal pieces of jewellery. Use a cocktail stick to apply the glue from the glue gun. The Tiara is intended to be worn around the Bun from the Hair in a Bun hairpiece on page 21.

GEMSTONE NECKLACE

■ A 1m length of Scheepjes Catona, Nude

■ A 2.5mm hook

■ Acrylic gems and rhinestones

■ 10cm of necklace chain and a necklace clasp (see Note)

■ 2 jump rings (from a jewellery supplier)

■ Craft glue

■ Wire cutters

■ Pliers

Note

You can cut an old necklace chain on each side of the clasp with wire cutters. Leave about 4cm of chain on each

side of the clasp then trim it to fit once you've tried it around Betty's neck.

Split the length of Nude in half. You'll need to do this slowly to avoid it tangling; untwist the main strand between thumb and finger as you pull it apart.

Using this strand and a 2.5mm hook, ch9 leaving a long starting tail.

Row 1 Dc in second ch from hook and in each ch to end, turn. [8 sts]

Row 2 Ch1, dc2tog, 4dc, dc2tog, turn. [6 sts]

Row 3 Ch1, dc2tog, 2dc, dc2tog, fasten off leaving a long tail.

Stick gemstones and rhinestones to this piece using the image as a guide. Use the starting and finishing tail to sew a jump ring to each of the top corners, and join the ends of the necklace chain to these.

CLUTCH BAG

■ Scheepjes Catona, Jet Black (10g)

■ A 3mm hook

■ Lining fabric (see note on page 11)

■ Beads or pieces of costume jewellery for fake fastening

■ Craft glue

■ Stitch marker

FRONT

With Jet Black and a 3mm hook, ch15.

Row 1 (RS) Dc in second ch from hook and in each

ch to end, turn. [14 sts]

Rows 2-3 Ch1, dc in each st to end, turn.

Row 4 Ch1, dc in each st to last 2 sts, dc2tog, turn. [13 sts]

Row 5 As Row 4. [12 sts]

Row 6 Ch1, dc in each st to end, turn.

Row 7 Skip first 2 dc, 4tr in next dc, tr in next 6 sts, 4tr in next st, ss in end of row, put live loop in a stitch marker and cut yarn leaving a 50cm tail.

BACK

Rejoin Jet Black to the other side of the foundation ch with RS facing.

Row 1 (RS) Ch1, dc in each st to end, turn.

Repeat Rows 2-7 of Front, do not fasten off.

*Ss in end of next 2 rows, dc in end of next 6 rows, ss in end of next 2 rows, fasten off leaving a long tail. Pick up the live loop from the Front and repeat from *, do not cut the end of yarn.

Use this piece as a template for the lining fabric, drawing round and cutting out the piece slightly smaller than the crochet fabric. Fold the lining fabric to match the fold in the Bag, then stick to the WS of the crochet piece. Run the end tails of yarn through the edging sts on each side as a gathering thread, pull up and secure to fold the Bag.

Sew a bead on each side of the Bag as a fake fastening and a loop of ribbon to attach Betty's hand.

betty's evening gown

Betty's always looking for an excuse to wear this dress. It needs a red carpet walk to make the most of the train, and the ribbon adds an extra touch of sophistication. The bare-shouldered look is complemented perfectly by her statement necklace

Materials

- Scheepjes Catona, Lilac Mist (75g)
- A 3mm hook
- 3 buttons, 5mm
- A press fastener
- 1m of sheer ribbon, 2.5cm wide
- Acrylic gems and rhinestones
- Craft glue
- Sewing thread

Note

The Skirt is worked from the waist down in rows, then the Body is worked from the foundation row of the Skirt up. The Train section is made separately from side to side in rows and sewn in to the back seam of the Gown.

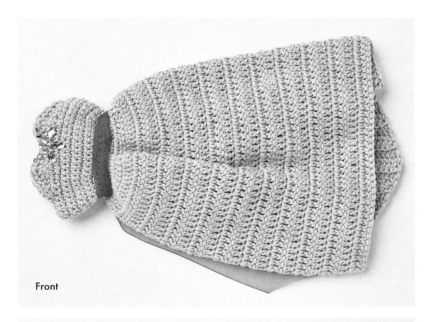

Front

Back

SKIRT

With Lilac Mist and a 3mm hook, ch26.

Row 1 (RS) Dc in second ch from hook and in each ch to end, turn, fasten off. [25 sts]

Change to a 2.5mm hook.

Row 2 Ch3 (counts as tr throughout), tr in same st, 2tr in each st to end, turn. [50 sts]

Row 3 Ch3, 2tr in next st, (tr in next st, 2tr in next st) to end, turn. [75 sts]

Rows 4-6 Ch3, tr in each st to end, turn.

Change to a 3mm hook.

Rows 7-22 Ch3, tr in each st to end, turn.

Fasten off leaving a long tail.

BODY

With Lilac Mist and a 3mm hook rejoin to the first st on the other side of the foundation ch of the Skirt with a dc and RS facing.

Row 1 (RS) Dc in each rem st of foundation ch to end, turn. [25 sts]

Row 2 Ch1, 4dc, 2dc in next st, 3dc, 2dc in next st, 7dc, 2dc in next st, 3dc, 2dc in next st, 4dc, turn. [29 sts]

Row 3 Ch1, (4dc, 2dc in next st) twice, 9dc, (2dc in next st, 4dc) twice, turn. [33 sts]

Row 4 Ch1, (5dc, 2dc in next st) twice, 9dc, (2dc in next st, 5dc) twice, turn. [37 sts]

Row 5 Ch1, 6dc, 2dc in next st, 5dc, 2dc in next st, 11dc, 2dc in next st, 5dc, 2dc in next st, 6dc, turn. [41 sts]

Row 6 Ch1, 10dc, 2dc in next st, 19dc, 2dc in next st, 10dc, turn. [43 sts]

Rows 7-9 Ch1, dc in each st to end, turn.

Row 10 Ch1, 16dc, htr in next st, 2tr in next st, htr in next st, 4dc, htr in next st, 2tr in next st, htr in next st, 17dc, [45 sts] rotate to work in row ends for buttonholes; dc in first row end, ch1, skip next row end (dc in next 2 row ends, ch1, skip next row end) twice, dc in next 2 row ends, fasten off. [3 buttonholes]

Rejoin Lilac Mist with RS facing in the 15th st of the next row with a ss.

Row 11 Dc in next st, *2htr, 2tr in next st, tr in next st, 2htr,** 2dc; rep from * to **, dc in next st, ss in next st, turn leaving rem sts unworked. [20 sts including ss]

Row 12 Skip ss, ss in next dc, *dc in next st, 2htr, 2htr in next st, 2htr, dc in next st, ss in next 2 sts; rep from * once more, turn. [21 sts including ss]

Row 13 Skip ss, dc in next ss, 3htr, 2htr in next st, 2htr, dc in next st, 4ss, dc in next st, 2htr, 2htr in next st, 3htr, dc in next st, ss in base of st at end of Row 11, ss in next unworked st, turn. [24 sts including ss]

Row 14 Skip ss, ss in next 23 sts, ss in next unworked st, fasten off.

TRAIN

With Lilac Mist and a 3mm hook, ch47 leaving a long starting tail.

Row 1 (WS) Ss in second ch from hook and in next 13 ch, dc in next 14ch, htr in next 9 ch, tr in next 9 ch, turn. [46 sts]

Work in back loops only throughout.

Row 2 (RS) Ch3 (counts as tr throughout), tr in st at base of ch, tr in each st to end, turn. [47 sts]

Row 3 Ch1, 14ss, 14dc, 9htr, tr in each st to last st, 2tr in last st, turn. [48 sts]

Rows 4-9 Repeat Rows 2-3. [54 sts after Row 9]

Row 10 Ch3, tr in each st to end, turn.

Row 11 Ch1, 14ss, 14dc, 9htr, tr in each st to last 2 sts, tr2tog, turn. [53 sts]

Row 12 Ch3, tr2tog, tr in each st to end, turn. [52 sts]

Rows 13-18 Repeat Rows 11-12. [46 sts after Row 18]

Row 19 Ch1, 14ss, 14dc, 9htr, 9tr.

Fasten off leaving a long tail.

Use buttons and a press fastener to fasten the Gown

Sew ribbon in position at the top of the Train

TO MAKE UP

See Evening Gown Train Diagram on page 127.
Fold the Train flat at the top, so that the two edges
meet at the centre back. Sew together across the top.
Sew the left edge of the Train to the long edge of the
Skirt on the left side. Run a gathering thread across
the folded top edge of the Train, pull up as much as
possible and secure. Sew this edge to the Waist of the
Gown on the left side, tucking in the corner at the top
left. On the right, you'll need to leave an opening to
get the Gown over Betty's hips, so sew the right edge
of the Train to the right edge of the Skirt from the hem
as far as Row 9 on the Skirt, or as far as you dare
go and still be able to remove the Gown! Check this
on Betty before fastening off. Sew a press fastener
underneath the top-right corner of the Train, with the
other side attached underneath the Waist on the right.
Sew 3 buttons opposite the buttonholes on the back
right edge of the Top.

Tie a bow with the ribbon, leaving ends that will
almost reach to the bottom of the Train when the bow
is attached at the top. Secure the bow with a few
stitches in sewing thread on the reverse, and sew to

Decorate the base of the Train with rhinestones

the top of the Train. Put a little glue on the raw edges
to seal. Fold the remainder of ribbon in half and sew
the edges together to make it half the width. Position
the seam of the ribbon at the centre back and sew to
the waistline with sewing thread, folding the ends of
the ribbon in to neaten the ends. Stick rhinestones to
the base of the Train, and the centre front of the Body,
using the image as a guide.

BERT'S 'OSCAT' TROPHY

- Gold lurex yarn (5g)
- A 2.5mm hook
- 2 cocktail sticks
- A plastic bottle cap
- Toy filling
- Craft glue
- Glue gun
- Craft knife

See note about decreasing on page 10.

BODY

With gold yarn and a 2.5mm hook, ch11 leaving a long starting tail.

Row 1 (RS) Dc in second ch from hook and in each ch to end, do not turn but work the first st of the next row from the RS to join into the round. [10 sts]

Work in a spiral in front loops only throughout.

Round 2 (2dc in next st, 1dc) twice, ch3, skip 3 sts, dc in next st, 2dc in next st, 1dc. [10 sts, ch-3 sp]

The ch-3 sp leaves a gap for the Front Leg Piece

which will be sewn on later.

Round 3 2dc, 2dc in next st, 3dc, dc in next 3 ch, 3dc, 2dc in next st. [15 sts]

Round 4 2dc, 2dc in next st, dc in each st to last st, 2dc in last st. [17 sts]

Round 5 Dc in each st around.

Round 6 2dc in first st, dc in each rem st around. [18 sts]

Round 7 Dc in each st around.

Round 8 (partial round for Tail) Dc to centre back, ch9, ss in second ch from hook and each ch back to Body, ss in base of ch, fasten off.

FRONT LEG PIECE

With gold yarn and a 2.5mm hook, ch9 leaving a long starting tail. Work in both loops of the stitch.

Row 1 Dc in second ch from hook and in each ch to end, turn. [8 sts]

Rows 2-3 Dc in each st to end, turn.

Fasten off leaving a long tail.

Fold the row ends under at one end of the piece and sew in place for the paws. At the opposite end, sew

the row ends to the top of the ch-3 sp in Round 2, leaving the opening behind so that you can insert cocktail sticks into this hole to reinforce the legs and neck. Sew the sides of this piece to the front of the Body with the paws at the bottom.

HEAD

With gold yarn and a 2.5mm hook, make a magic loop leaving a long starting tail.

Round 1 (RS) Ch1, 6dc into loop, continue working in a spiral in front loops only. [6 sts]

Round 2 (2dc in next st, 2dc) twice. [8 sts]

Round 3 (2dc in next st, 3dc) twice. [10 sts]

Rounds 4-5 Dc in each st around.

Round 6 (Dec, 3dc) twice, do not fasten off.

Thread a needle with the starting tail of yarn and pass from the inside to the outside of the Head in the first ear position. Sew a couple of small loops of yarn in this position, and secure with a couple of stitches to make an ear. Take the yarn back to the inside of the Head and repeat in the other ear position, fasten off.

Put some filling inside the Head through the Round 6 opening, then cut yarn and run the tail around the rem sts to gather and pull closed. Fasten off and weave in ends.

TO MAKE UP

Cut the cocktail sticks to approx 4.5cm in length using the craft knife, leaving the pointed ends of the sticks on one end. The sticks should be long enough to reach to the bottom of the paws, leave a length of 0.5cm for the neck and enter the Head without sticking through the top. Insert the blunt ends of the cocktail sticks through the neck opening, through the hole left by the ch-3 sp on the Body and down the Front Leg Piece. Put some craft glue on the pointed ends and insert them into the base of the Head. Put some more glue on the neck space of the sticks and wind the starting tail of the Body around the sticks to cover the gap. Use more glue to seal the end of the yarn in place.

Put some stuffing inside the Body and use the glue gun to stick the Body to the top of the bottle cap as the base for the Trophy.

BERT'S BOWTIE

- ■ Scheepjes Catona, Lilac Mist (5g)
- ■ A 3mm hook
- ■ Button, 5mm
- ■ Acrylic rhinestones
- ■ Craft glue

COLLAR

With Lilac Mist and a 3mm hook, ch13.

Row 1 Dc in second ch from hook and in each ch to end, ch4, ss in end of row to form a button loop, fasten off and weave in ends.

Sew a button onto the end of the Collar on the opposite end from the button loop.

BOW

With Lilac Mist and a 3mm hook, ch9.

Row 1 Dc in second ch from hook and in each ch to end, turn. [8 sts]

Rows 2-3 Ch1, dc in each st to end, turn.

Fasten off leaving a long tail.

TO MAKE UP

Use the tail of yarn to sew a stitch to pinch the centre of the Bow. Wrap the end of yarn around the centre a few times and secure on the back of the Bow with a stitch, then sew the Bow to the centre of the Collar. Stick rhinestones to the Bow with craft glue.

chapter five:
betty goes on holiday

Just imagine the scene: glorious sunshine, an open top Chevy, the Pacific Coast Highway and Betty with her headscarf to keep her hairdo neat in the wind. She has her swimsuit packed in her beach bag ready for some serious sunbathing. Bert, on the other hand, prefers to keep his feet on the ground! He can just about cope with a car journey if he's lying down in his basket

Total yarn quantities for this section: Scheepjes Catona 5g of Cyan (397), 45g of Candy Apple (516), 30g of Snow White (106), 40g of Jet Black (110), 20g of Chocolate (507), 35g of Apple Granny (513), 30cm length of Soft Rose (409). Check the yarn quantities needed for all projects on page 121.

holiday packing

Betty's given a lot of thought to what would make the perfect capsule wardrobe for her holiday. Her stylish capri pants are just the thing for driving, and her neat little top will take her from the beach to a drink at a nearby diner

Materials
■ Scheepjes Catona, Cyan (15g)

■ A 3mm hook

■ 7 buttons, 5mm

See note about decreasing on page 10.

Note
The Top is worked from the bottom up in one piece to the armholes, then worked for part of the row to form the Left Front and Back. The yarn is then rejoined on the remaining unworked sts for the Right Front and Back.

SLEEVELESS TOP

Front

BODY
With Cyan and a 3mm hook, ch26.
Row 1 (RS) Ch1, dc in each ch to end, turn. [25 sts]
Row 2 Ch1, 4dc, 2dc in next st, 3dc, 2dc in next st, 7dc, 2dc in next st, 3dc, 2dc in next st, 4dc, turn. [29 sts]
Row 3 Ch1, (4dc, 2dc in next st) twice, 9dc, (2dc in next st, 4dc) twice, turn. [33 sts]
Row 4 Ch1, (5dc, 2dc in next st) twice, 9dc, (2dc in next st, 5dc) twice, turn. [37 sts]
Row 5 Ch1, 6dc, 2dc in next st, 5dc, 2dc in next st, 11dc, 2dc in next st, 5dc, 2dc in next st, 6dc, turn. [41 sts]
Row 6 Ch1, 10dc, 2dc in next st, 19dc, 2dc in next st, 10dc, turn. [43 sts]
Rows 7-10 Ch1, dc in each st to end, turn.

Back

Left Front and Back

Row 11 Ch1, 8dc, ch9, skip next 5 sts on Body, dc in next 8 sts, ss in next st, turn leaving rem sts unworked. [8dc for Back, 8dc for Front, 9 ch for armhole]

Row 12 Skip ss, dc in each st, dc in back of each ch for armhole and each rem dc, turn. [25 sts]

Row 13 Ch1, 7dc, dec, 8dc, dec, 6dc, turn. [23 sts]

Row 14 Ch1, (6dc, dec) twice, 7dc, turn. [21 sts]

Row 15 Ch1, 7dc, dec, 4dc, dec, 6dc, turn. [19 sts]

Row 16 Ch1, 7dc, dec, 2dc, dec, 6dc, turn. [17 sts]

Row 17 Ch1, 6dc, dec, 2dc, dec, 5dc, turn. [15 sts]

Row 18 Ch1, 5dc, dec, 2dc, dec, 4dc, turn. [13 sts]

Row 19 Ch1, 6dc, dec, 5dc, turn. [12 sts]

Row 20 Ch1, 8dc in back loops only, 4dc, turn.

Row 21 Ch1, 4dc, 8dc in front loops only (to encourage the collar to roll), do not fasten off.

Rotate to work down row ends for buttonholes as follows:

Dc in first row end, ch1, skip next row end, (dc in next 2 row ends, ch1, skip next row end) 6 times, dc in next row end, fasten off. [7 ch-1 buttonholes]

Right Front and Back

With RS facing, rejoin yarn with a ss in same ss at centre Front on Row 11 of Left Front and Back.

Row 11 Dc in next 8 sts, ch9, skip next 5 sts on Body, dc in next 8 sts. [8dc for Back, 8dc for Front, 9 ch for armhole]

Row 12 Ch1, dc in each st, dc in back of each ch for armhole and each rem dc, skip ss, turn. [25 sts]

Rows 13-19 Repeat Rows 13-19 of Left Front and Back.

Row 20 Ch1, 4dc, 8dc in back loops only, turn.

Row 21 Ch1, 8dc in front loops only, 4dc, fasten off.

TO FINISH

Use the tail of yarn to sew down the point of the collar. Sew down the point of the collar on the other side. Sew buttons to Right Back to correspond with buttonholes on Left Back.

Weave in all ends.

CAPRI PANTS

Materials
- Scheepjes Catona, Jet Black (15g)
- Scheepjes Catona, Snow White (15g)
- A 3mm hook
- Button, 5mm

Note
See Capri Pants Chart on page 128.

The Capri Pants are worked in rows from side to side, with shaping at the waistline edge worked by using slip stitches to narrow the waist. The increases are worked by adding extra ch at the beginning or end of the row as appropriate, then working into this extension ch on the following row. In the (dc, ch1) rib pattern, ch always count as sts.

A row of Jet Black and a row of Snow White are worked from the RS, then a row of Jet Black and Snow White are worked from the WS. Take care to watch the turning instructions at the end of each row. This pattern continues throughout.

At the beginning of the pattern you'll need to fasten off after the first 2 rows. After that, carry the yarn and

Front

Back

do not fasten off. As you're working two rows from the RS followed by two rows from the WS, you'll need to leave a live working loop at the end of the row. You can put a stitch marker in this loop if you wish to stop it pulling out, otherwise just pull up a long loop to guard against it pulling through. To pick up the colour again next time it's needed, insert the hook into the first st at the beg of the row, then through the live loop and pull it through the first st before starting the row instructions.

LEG

Worked from the centre back.
With Jet Black and a 3mm hook, ch24.

Row 1 (RS) Dc in second ch from hook, ch1, skip next ch, dc in next ch, (ch1, skip next ch, dc in next ch) to end, ch2 as extension for next row, fasten off, do not turn. [23 sts plus ch-2]

Row 2 (RS) With Snow White, dc in first st, (ch1, skip next ch, dc in next dc) repeat to end, working last dc in the second ch of the extension ch, ch2 as extension for next row, fasten off, turn. [25 sts plus ch-2]

Row 3 (WS) With Jet Black, ch4 as extension for next row, dc in first ch of extension from Row 2, ch1, skip next ch, dc in next dc, (ch1, skip next ch, dc in next dc) repeat to end, do not turn. [27 sts plus ch-4]

Row 4 (WS) With Snow White, ch4 as extension for

next row, dc in first ch of extension from Row 3, ch1, skip next ch, dc in next ch, ch1, skip next ch, dc in next dc, (ch1, skip next ch, dc in next dc) to last 8 sts, ss in back loops only of last 8 sts, turn. [31 sts plus ch-4]

Row 5 (RS) Pick up Jet Black, ch1, ss in back loops only of first 8 sts, dc in next st, (ch1, skip next ch, dc in next dc) to end working last 4 sts in extension ch as before, ch4 as extension for next row, do not turn. [35 sts plus ch-4]

Row 6 (RS) Pick up Snow White and repeat Row 5. Once the last st has been worked in the last ch of the extension ch, insert the hook into the Jet Black loop as well, and holding both Jet Black and Snow White together to carry the yarn to the right position for following rows, work the extension ch4, turn. [39 sts plus ch-4]

Row 7 (WS) Drop the Snow White loop and leaving Jet Black only, ch1, dc in first st of extension ch, ch1, skip next ch, dc in next ch, ch1, skip next ch, dc in next dc, (ch1, skip next ch, dc in next dc) to last 8 sts, ss in back loops only of last 8 sts, do not turn. [43 sts]

Row 8 (WS) Pick up Snow White, ch1, dc in first dc, (ch1, skip next ch, dc in next dc) to last 8 sts, ss in back loops only of last 8 sts, turn.

Row 9 (RS) Pick up Jet Black, ch1, dc in first st, (ch1, skip next st, dc in next st) to end, do not turn.

Row 10 (RS) Pick up Snow White, ch1, dc in first st, (ch1, skip next st, dc in next st) to end, turn.

Rows 11-14 Repeat the last 2 rows twice more, working the first 2 rows from the WS and the second 2 rows from the RS.

Rows 15-16 (WS) As Row 8 with Jet Black then Snow White, turn after Row 16.

Row 17 (RS) Pick up Jet Black, ch1, ss in back loops only of first 8 sts, dc in next dc, (ch1, skip next ch, dc in next dc) to end, do not turn.

Row 18 (RS) As Row 17 with Snow White, turn.

Row 19 (WS) As Row 8 with Jet Black, do not turn.

Row 20 (WS) Pick up Snow White, ch1, dc in first st, (ch1, skip next st, dc in next st) to end, turn.

Rows 21-22 (RS) As Row 20 with Jet Black then Snow White, fasten off leaving a long tail.

Row 23 (WS) Rejoin Jet Black to the 23rd st from the waistline edge with a ss. (Ch1, skip next st, dc in next st) to end, fasten off and weave in ends. [23 sts]

Fold the Leg RS together, and use the ending tail to sew the inside Leg seam, leaving 21 sts open at the top.

Repeat for the second Leg, reversing the colours so that you start with Snow White and end with Jet Black. The RS and WS will also be reversed for the second Leg, but this only matters once you're sewing up. Flip the second Leg piece over to the other side to make sure it mirrors the first piece.

Align centre front seam of both pieces and sew. Sew centre back seam from crotch upwards, leaving 13 sts open at the top.

WAISTBAND
Rejoin Jet Black at left side of waistline top edge with RS facing.

Row 1 (RS) Ch1, work 30dc evenly around the top edge, turn. [30 sts]

Row 2 Ch1, dc in first st, dc2tog, (4dc, dc2tog) 4 times, 3dc, turn. [25 sts]

Row 3 Ch1, dc in each st to end, ch4 to make a button loop and ss to bottom edge of Waistband. Fasten off and weave in ends.

Sew the button to side of Waistband opposite the button loop.

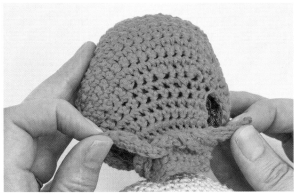

HEAD SCARF
Materials
▢ Scheepjes Catona, Candy Apple (15g)

▢ A 3mm hook

Note
The Head Scarf is made from two pieces; a Main Piece and a Necktie. The Necktie is sewn to the row ends of the Main Piece at the front. The back of the Main Piece is left open so that you can take the Head Scarf on and off. The Necktie

is tied at the back and there is a flap on the back of the Main Piece which tucks underneath the Necktie. The Hair Piece for Head Scarf on page 64 is intended to be worn underneath the Head Scarf, as it isn't bulky at the top.

MAIN PIECE
With Candy Apple and a 3mm hook, ch41.
Row 1 (RS) Dc in second ch from hook and in each ch to end, turn. [40 sts]
Row 2 Ch1, dc in each st to end, turn.
Row 3 Ch1, 7dc in back loops only, dc in both loops to last 7 sts, 7dc in back loops only, turn.
Rows 4-6 Ch1, dc in each st to end, turn.
Row 7 Insert hook in the remaining front loop of Row 2 and the front loop of Row 7 at the same time and complete a dc stitch. Repeat for the next 6 sts, using each of the loops from Row 2. Dc in each st as normal to last 7 sts, then insert hook in the 2 front loops for the last 7 dc as before, turn.
Row 8 Ch1, dc in each st to end, turn.
Row 9 Ch1, 11dc in back loops only, dc in both loops to last 11 sts, 11dc in back loops only, turn.
Rows 10-12 Ch1, dc in each st to end, turn.
Row 13 Insert hook in 2 front loops for first 11 sts as before, dc in each st as normal to last 11 sts, insert hook in 2 front loops for last 11 sts, turn.
Row 14 Ch1, dc2tog, 7dc, (dc2tog, 2dc) 5 times, dc2tog, 7dc, dc2tog, turn. [32 sts]
Row 15 Ch1, dc2tog, 6dc, (dc2tog, 2dc) twice, (2dc, dc2tog) twice, 6dc, dc2tog, fasten off. [26 sts]
Rejoin yarn with WS facing in the 8th st of the row.
Row 16 Ch1, 12dc, turn leaving remaining sts unworked. [12 sts]
Row 17 Ch1, dc in each st to end, turn.
Row 18 Ch1, 2dc in first st, dc in each st to last st, 2dc in last st, turn. [14 sts]
Rows 19-21 Ch1, dc in each st to end, turn.
Row 22 Ch1, dc2tog, dc in each st to last 2 sts, dc2tog, turn. [12 sts]
Row 23 As Row 22, fasten off and weave in ends. [10 sts]

NECKTIE

With Candy Apple and a 3mm hook, ch42.

Round 1 (RS) Ss in second ch from hook, ss in next ch, dc in each ch to last 2 sts, ss in last 2 ch, ch1 and rotate to work in the opposite side of the foundation ch, ss in next 2 sts, dc in each st to last 2 sts, ss in last 2 sts, fasten off and weave in ends.

TO MAKE UP

See Head Scarf Diagram on page 129.

Bring the row ends of Rows 1 and 2 on the Main Piece together to sew into a tube, leaving the rest of the row ends open. Find the mid-point of the Necktie and align it with the front centre seam just made. Run a gathering thread across the remaining row ends and draw up slightly, so that when you sew one side of the Necktie to the row ends of the Main Piece it takes up a total of 9 sts on the Necktie. To fit the Head Scarf, put it over Betty's head using the opening at the back and tie the Necktie at the back, tucking the flap underneath.

HAIR PIECE FOR HEAD SCARF
Materials
- Scheepjes Catona, Chocolate (15g)
- A 3mm hook
- Black shirring elastic and a piece of hook and loop fastening if you want the hair to be removable

Note
There are five pieces which make up this Hair Piece. The main piece is the Hair Cap which fits over the back of the head. There are two pieces for the front, a larger piece which goes on Betty's right and a shorter piece on Betty's left. There are two identical pieces for the back.

HAIR CAP

With Chocolate and a 3mm hook, ch17, leaving a long starting tail.

Row 1 (RS) Htr in second ch from hook (skipped ch does not count as st), htr in next ch, 4dc, 4ss, 4dc, 2htr, turn. [16 sts]

Now working in back loops only:

Row 2 Ch1, 2htr, 4dc, 4ss, dc in each st to last 2 sts, 1htr, 2htr in last st, turn. [17 sts]

Row 3 Ch1, htr in each htr, dc in each dc, ss in each ss to end, turn.

Rows 4-7 Repeat Rows 2-3 twice more. [19 sts after Row 7]

Row 8 Ch1, htr in each htr, dc in each dc, ss in each ss to last 2 sts, htr2tog, turn. [18 sts]

Row 9 Ch1, 3htr, dc in each dc, ss in each ss, htr in each htr to end, turn.

Rows 10-11 Repeat Rows 8-9. [17 sts]

Row 12 As Row 8. [16 sts]

Row 13 Ch1, 2htr, dc in each dc, ss in each ss, htr in each htr, fasten off leaving a long tail.

Using the long tails, sew the first half of the foundation ch to the second half, and the first half of the last row to the second half, as shown in the Hair Piece Diagram on page 129. The back of the Hair Cap is the row ends with the increases.

RIGHT FRONT PIECE

With Chocolate and a 3mm hook, ch11 leaving a long starting tail.

Row 1 (WS) Dc in second ch from hook and in each ch to end, turn. [10 sts]

Now working in back loops only:

Rows 2-3 Ch1, dc in each st to end, turn.

Row 4 Ch1, dc in each st to last st, 2dc in last st, turn. [11 sts]

Row 5 Ch1, dc in each st to end, turn.

Rows 6-11 Repeat Rows 4-5 three more times. [14 sts after Row 11]

Fasten off leaving a long tail.

LEFT FRONT PIECE

With Chocolate and a 3mm hook, ch7.

Row 1 (WS) Dc in second ch from hook and in each ch to end, turn. [6 sts]

Now working in back loops only:
Rows 2-3 Ch1, dc in each st to end, turn.
Row 4 Ch1, dc in each st to last st, 2dc in last st, turn. [7 sts]
Row 5 Ch1, dc in each st to end, turn.
Rows 6-9 Repeat Rows 4-5 twice more. [9 sts after Row 9]
Fasten off leaving a long tail.

BACK (MAKE 2)

With Chocolate and a 3mm hook, ch3 leaving a long starting tail.
Row 1 (RS) Dc in second ch from hook and next ch, turn. [2 sts]
Now working in back loops only:
Row 2 Ch1, 2dc in first st, dc in next st, turn. [3 sts]
Row 3 Ch1, 2dc, 2dc in last st, turn. [4 sts]
Row 4 Ch1, 2dc in first st, 2dc, 2dc in last st, turn. [6 sts]
Row 5 Ch1, dc in each st to end, turn.
Row 6 Ch1, 2dc in first st, dc in each st to last st, 2dc in last st. [8 sts]
Rows 7-9 Ch1, dc in each st to last st, 2dc in last st, turn. [11 sts after Row 9]
Row 10 As Row 6. [13 sts]
Row 11 As Row 7. [14 sts]
Fasten off leaving a long tail.

TO MAKE UP

See Hair Piece Diagram on page 129.
Curl the front corner of the Right Front piece over and sew in position. Repeat for the Corner of the Left Front piece and sew the Right Front to the Left for approx 1cm as shown in the Diagram. Pin or tack the joined Front pieces around the front of the Hair Cap, curling under the corner on the Right Front piece.

Include the row ends of that piece in the join to the Hair Cap, leaving 2 rows at the end unsewn.
Curl up the corner of one Back piece and sew in position. Run a gathering thread along the joining edge and pull up so that the piece will fit from the Ear to the centre back of the Hair Cap. Sew just underneath the edge of the Hair Cap. Flip the other Back piece over and repeat.

Sew the Hair Piece to Betty's Head if you want it to be fixed. If you want removable hair, run a length of shirring elastic around the inside edge of the Hair Piece and pull up slightly before securing. Sew a piece of hook and loop fastening on the inside top to correspond with the piece on Betty's Head (see instructions for the Head on page 20).

betty's swimsuit

Sunbathing is more Betty's thing than swimming because she really doesn't like getting her hair wet! This swimsuit is as much about showing off her fashion sense as it is her figure; the contrast piping and button detail make her look the part

Materials

- Scheepjes Catona, Candy Apple (20g)
- Scheepjes Catona, Snow White (5g)
- A 3mm hook
- 3 buttons, 5mm
- 2 press fasteners

See note about decreasing on page 10.

Note

The Swimsuit is worked from the bottom up in one piece, with an overlap on one side so that you can remove it. The bottom of the overlap piece is sewn down afterwards, and a gusset strip is worked from the foundation ch at the front and then sewn onto the back.

With Candy Apple and a 3mm hook, ch41, leaving a long starting tail.

Row 1 (WS) Dc in second ch from hook and in each ch to end, turn. [40 sts]

Rows 2-8 Ch1, dc in each st to end, turn.

Row 9 Ch1, dec, dc in each st to last 2 sts, dec, turn. [38 sts]

Row 10 Ch1, dc in each st to end, turn.

Row 11 Ch1, (11dc, dec) twice, 12dc, turn. [36 sts]

Row 12 Ch1, 5dc, dec, 22dc, dec, 5dc, turn. [34 sts]

Row 13 Ch1, 9dc, dec, 12dc, dec, 9dc, turn. [32 sts]

Row 14 Ch1, 5dc, dec, 18dc, dec, 5dc, turn. [30 sts]

Row 15 Ch1, dc in each st to end, turn.

Row 16 Ch1, 8dc, 2dc in next st, 4dc, 2dc in next st, 8dc, 2dc in next st, 4dc, 2dc in next st, 2dc, turn. [34 sts]

Rows 17-19 Ch1, dc in each st to end, turn.

Row 20 Ch1, (6dc, 2dc in next st) 4 times, 6dc, turn. [38 sts]

Row 21 Ch1, 5dc, (2dc in next st, 7dc) 4 times, 1dc, turn. [42 sts]

Row 22 Ch1, dc in each st to end, turn.

Row 23 Ch1, (8dc, 2dc in next st) 4 times, 6dc, turn. [46 sts]

Row 24 Ch1, dc in each st to end, turn, do not fasten off.

CUPS

See Swimsuit Cups Chart on page 129.

Row 25 (WS) Ch1, dc in each st to last 13 sts, 1htr, 2tr in next st, 1htr, 4dc, 1htr, 2tr in next st, 1htr, 3dc, turn. [48 sts]

Row 26 (RS) Ch1, *2dc, 2htr, 2tr in next st, 1tr, 2htr; rep from * once more, dc in next st, 1ss, turn leaving rem sts unworked. [20 sts including ss]

Row 27 Skip ss, ss in next dc, *1dc, 2htr, 2htr in next st, 2htr, dc in next st, ss in next 2 sts; rep from * once more, turn. [21 sts including ss]

Row 28 Skip ss, dc in next ss, 2htr, 1tr, 2tr in next st, 1tr, 1htr, 1dc, 4ss, 1dc, 1htr, 1tr, 2tr in next st, 1tr, 2htr, 1dc, ss in base of st at end of Row 26, fasten off. [23 sts including ss]

GUSSET

With RS facing and the 'Cup' end of the Suit towards you, count back 7 sts along the foundation ch from the left edge, and rejoin Candy Apple with a 3mm hook in the 7th st.

Row 1 (RS) Ch1, dc in other side of foundation ch for 3 sts, turn. [3 sts]

Row 2 Ch1, dc in first st, skip next st, dc in last st, turn. [2 sts]

Rows 3-7 Ch1, dc in each st to end, turn. Adjust the total number of rows if necessary by checking the fit on Betty.

Row 8 Ch1, 2dc in first st, dc in next st, fasten off leaving a long tail.

TO MAKE UP

See Swimsuit Diagram on page 129.

Fold the front edge of the Swimsuit with the Cups on top, so that the first 2 and last 2 sts overlap. Sew the overlapping front edge in place, stitching up the front edge for about four rows.

Use the finishing tail to sew the Gusset to the central back 3 sts of the Suit, so that there are 16 sts for each leg.

TO FINISH

Make a slip knot in the end of Snow White, insert the hook in the bottom front edge from front to back and pull the slip knot through. Work a line of ss surface crochet up the front edge and around the top of the Cups, ending at the end of the second Cup. Work another line of ss crochet inside the first along the top edge of the Cups, using the top of Row 27 where possible, fasten off. Sew the buttons on the front edge at the waist, using the image as a guide.

Sew a press fastener underneath the overlap at the waist, making sure to pull the waist in as much as possible. Sew another fastener at the top corner.

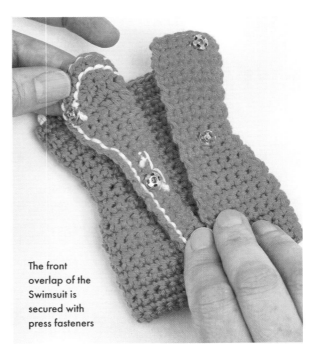

The front overlap of the Swimsuit is secured with press fasteners

BALLET FLATS
Materials

■ Scheepjes Catona, Candy Apple (5g)

■ A 2.5mm hook

SOLE AND UPPER

The Sole and Upper is the same as the Sole and Upper of the Dancing Shoes on page 104, up to the end of Round 3. Round 4 is as follows:

Round 4 Ss tightly in each st around, fasten off and weave in ends.

Continue to the finishing instructions below.

TO FINISH

Cut a length of Candy Apple and split it in half. Tie a small bow with each piece and trim the ends. Paint the bows with craft glue to stiffen them and stick one to the front of each shoe.

BEACH BAG

Materials

■ Scheepjes Catona, Candy Apple (5g)

■ Scheepjes Catona, Snow White (10g)

■ A 3mm hook

Note

The Front and Back pieces are worked in the round, closing off each round with a ss. When you change colours, change on the yrh of the ss. The increases in the circles are staggered to make an even circle shape. The Bag Gusset is worked onto the second Front/Back piece without fastening off, and then sewn to the first piece. An edging and Handles are worked onto the opening at the top of the Bag.

FRONT AND BACK (MAKE 2)

With Candy Apple and a 3mm hook, make a magic loop.

Round 1 (RS) Ch1, 6dc into loop, ss to first dc to join, changing to Snow White. [6 sts]

Round 2 Ch1, 2dc in each st around, ss to first dc, changing to Candy Apple. [12 sts]

Round 3 Ch1, dc in first st, 2dc in next st, (1dc, 2dc in next st) around, ss to first dc, changing to Snow White. [18 sts]

Round 4 Ch1, (2dc, 2dc in next st) 6 times, ss to first dc, changing to Candy Apple. [24 sts]

Round 5 Ch1, dc in first st, 2dc in next st, (3dc, 2dc in next st) around to last 2 sts, dc in last 2 sts, ss to first dc, changing to Snow White. [30 sts]

Round 6 Ch1, (4dc, 2dc in next st) around, ss to first dc, changing to Candy Apple. [36 sts]

Round 7 Ch1, 2dc, 2dc in next st, (5dc, 2dc in next st) around to last 3 sts, dc in last 3 sts, ss to first dc, changing to Snow White. [42 sts]

Round 8 Ch1, (6dc, 2dc in next st) around, ss to first dc, fasten off first piece and make another the same. At the end of the second piece do not fasten off and continue to Bag Gusset. [48 sts]

BAG GUSSET

Row 1 (RS) Ch1, working in back loops only, dc in next 32 sts, turn leaving rem sts unworked. [32 sts]

Rows 2-3 Ch1, dc in each st to end, turn.

Fasten off leaving a long tail.

Use the long tail to sew the Gusset to the back loops of 32 sts around the edge of the other piece.

This leaves an opening of 16 sts at the top on each of Front and Back.

HANDLES

Ss around the top opening edge as follows:

Rejoin Snow White to the fourth st from the right hand edge on the opening. Ss in each st of the opening on one side, the top edge of the Gusset, each opening st on the other side, the top of the Gusset and in each opening st back to the first st, ss in same st to join, do not fasten off.

*Ch21, skip next 6 sts on opening, ss in next st inserting hook right through piece from front to back, ss in same place on inside edge only to secure, dc in back of each ch, ss at base of ch, fasten off.**

Rejoin Snow White to fourth st from the right hand edge of opening on the other side, rep from * to **.

Weave in ends.

lying down bert & his travel basket

Bert is most at home when he's horizontal, and he definitely needs to be lying down when he journeys in his travel basket. Betty knows that he's not too keen, so she's got the best basket, complete with mouse-lined interior and brass finishings

Materials

- Scheepjes Catona, Jet Black (25g)
- A 30cm length of Scheepjes Catona, Soft Rose
- 2 30cm lengths of Scheepjes Catona, Snow White
- A 2.5mm hook
- Pipe cleaner, 30cm long
- Old black tights to use as filling
- Craft glue

See note about decreasing on page 10.

Measurements

Bert measures 10cm long and 7cm tall.

Note

The Body is made in two separate sections. The Neck/Front Body is worked from the Neck down, and the Back Body is worked from this piece towards the Tail.

LYING-DOWN BERT
NECK/FRONT BODY

With Jet Black and a 2.5mm hook, ch10 leaving a long starting tail, ss to first ch, being careful not to twist.

Round 1 (RS) Ch1, dc in each ch around. [10 sts].
Work in a spiral in front loops only.
Rounds 2-3 Dc in each st around.
Round 4 2dc in first st, dc in each rem st around. [11 sts]
Round 5 As Round 4. [12 sts]
Round 6 (2dc in next st, dc in next st) 6 times. [18 sts]
Round 7 Dc in each st around.
Round 8 4dc, 2dc in next st, 8dc, 2dc in next st, 4dc. [20 sts]
Round 9 Dc in each st around.
Round 10 5dc, 2dc in next st, 8dc, 2dc in next st, 5dc, do not fasten off. [22 sts]
The Legs are worked back and forth in rows on each side of Round 10, with a small extension ch to make them finish forward of the Body:

First Front Leg

Work in both loops of each stitch.
Row 11 7dc, ch5, turn.
Row 12 Dc in second ch from hook and next 7 sts, turn leaving rem sts unworked. [8 sts]
Rows 13-14 Ch1, dc in each st to end, turn.
Fasten off leaving a long tail.

Second Front Leg

Work in both loops of each stitch.
With Jet Black and a 2.5mm hook, ch4 leaving a long starting tail then work the next st into Round 10 as follows:
Row 1 (RS) Skip the next 8 unworked sts of Round 10 on the Neck/Front, dc in next 4 sts of Round 10, turn.
Row 2 Ch1, dc in next 4 sts and next 4 ch, turn. [8 sts]

Rows 3-4 Ch1, dc in each st to end, turn. Fasten off.

Use the tail on each Leg to sew the first and last row of the leg together, for the front four stitches only. See Bert's Legs Diagram on page 128.

BACK BODY

Foundation Round With Jet Black and a 2.5mm hook, ch6 and with RS facing dc in the first row end of the First Leg, at the back. See Bert's Back Body Diagram on page 128.

Dc in each rem row end of the First Leg (4dc in total), ch6, with RS facing dc in last row end of Second Leg and each rem row (4dc in total), ch6, ss to first ch being careful not to twist. This will give you a joined round made up of 12ch at the centre top, 4dc along the end of one leg, 6 ch along the bottom and 4dc along the end of the other leg. [26 sts]

The Back will be worked in the round on these sts, and will be sewn to the Neck/Front Body later.

Round 1 (RS) Ch1, dc in each st and ch around. [26 sts]

Round 2 4dc, 2dc in next st, 16dc, 2dc in next st, 4dc. [28 sts]

Rounds 3-4 Dc in each st around.

Round 5 5dc, 2dc in next st, 16dc, 2dc in next st, 5dc. [30 sts]

Rounds 6-7 Dc in each st around.

At this point, the beginning of the round needs to be aligned centrally with the Neck, so now work as many dc as it takes to make the new start of the round line up with the Neck. It will probably only take one or two.

Round 8 10dc, ch3, skip next st, 8dc, ch3, skip next st, 10dc. [28 dc and 2 ch-3 sps to make holes for the Back Paws]

Round 9 Dc in each st and ch around. [34 sts]

Round 10 2dc, dec, 1dc, dec, 20dc, dec, 1dc, dec, 2dc. [30 sts]

Round 11 (2dc, dec) 3 times, 6dc, (dec, 2dc) 3 times. [24 sts]

Round 12 (1dc, dec) 3 times, 6dc, (dec, 1dc) 3 times. [18 sts]

Round 13 (1dc, dec) 3 times, (dec, 1dc) 3 times. [12 sts]

Round 14 (Dec) 6 times, do not fasten off. [6 sts]

Tail

Work in both loops of each stitch.

Row 15 Ch1, dc in next 4 sts, turn leaving rem sts unworked. [4 sts]

Rows 16-26 Ch1, 4dc, turn.

Row 27 Ch1, dec, dc in each st to end, turn. [3 sts]

Row 28 Ch1, dec, dc in last st, fasten off leaving a long tail.

Use the tail of yarn to sew together the two row ends of the tail. If you wish you can sew the beginning of the tail to the Body once the Body has been stuffed, so leave the tail of yarn here for that purpose.

BACK PAWS (MAKE 2)

With Jet Black and a 2.5mm hook, make a magic loop.

Round 1 (RS) Ch1, 6dc into loop. [6 sts]

Round 2 Dc in each st around, fasten off leaving a long tail.

HEAD

Make as for Sitting-up Bert on page 39.

FRONT FLAP

This flap will fold underneath Bert and be sewn to the inside of the Legs and the unworked edge of the Back Body.

Rejoin Jet Black with a 2.5mm hook and RS facing to the first of the unworked 8 sts on Round 10 of the Neck/Front Body.

Row 1 (RS) Ch1, dc2tog, dc in each st to last 2 sts, dc2tog, turn. [6 sts]

Row 2 As Row 1. [4 sts]

Row 3 Ch1, dc in each st to end, turn.

Row 4 Ch1, 2dc in first st, 2dc, 2dc in last st, turn. [6 sts]

Row 5 Ch1, dc in each st to end, fasten off leaving a long tail.

TO MAKE UP

Take the pipe cleaner and fold in the same way as the one used for Sitting-up Bert. Put the folded ends down through the hole for the neck, and put each end inside one of the Front Leg pieces. Using pieces of the tights cut up, stuff the Neck/Front Body from the underside.

Before finishing the stuffing, sew the Front Flap to the underside as shown in the Front Flap Diagram on page 128, leaving a small opening to complete the stuffing before closing.

Use pieces of tights to stuff the Back Body. Before finishing the stuffing, sew the unworked foundation edge of the Back Body to the Front/Neck Body leaving a small opening, complete the stuffing and close.

Weave in all ends.

Sew the Back Paws in place to the ch-3 holes on the underside, sew the Head in place on the Neck following the instructions for Sitting-up Bert. Split a strand of Snow White in half to use to sew 3 straight stitches on each Paw.

BERT'S TRAVEL BASKET

Materials
- Scheepjes Catona, Apple Granny (35g)
- Scheepjes Catona, Chocolate (5g)
- A 2.5mm hook
- A 3mm hook
- 50cm of Kreinik gold wired braid
- 2 pipe cleaners, 30cm long
- 3 brass paper fasteners
- Darice 7 HPI ultra-stiff plastic canvas
- Lining fabric, approx 21x18cm (see note on page 11)
- Craft glue
- Sewing thread
- Craft knife
- Wire cutters

Note
The Travel Basket is made from 3 pieces; Back, Base and Top. These are sewn together, lined for strength and the front opening is reinforced with covered pipe cleaners. When working the Top piece, take care to keep the tension even.

BASE
With Apple Granny and a 3mm hook, ch22.
Row 1 (RS) Dc in second ch from hook and in each ch to end, turn. [21 sts]
Rows 2-15 Ch1, dc in each st to end, turn.
Fasten off leaving a long tail.

BACK
This is worked from the centre out, by working along both sides of the foundation ch.
With Apple Granny and a 3mm hook, ch12.
Row 1 (RS) Dc in second ch from hook and in each ch to last ch, 3dc in last ch, rotate to work along opposite side of foundation ch, dc in rem 10 sts, turn. [23 sts]
Row 2 Ch1, dc in first 10 sts, 2dc in next 3 sts, dc in last 10 sts, turn. [26 sts]
Row 3 Ch1, dc in first 10 sts, (1dc, 2dc in next st) 3 times, dc in last 10 sts, turn. [29 sts]
Row 4 Ch1, dc in first 10 sts, (2dc, 2dc in next st) 3 times, dc in last 10 sts, turn. [32 sts]
Row 5 Ch1, dc in first 10 sts, (3dc, 2dc in next st) 3 times, dc in last 10 sts, turn. [35 sts]
Row 6 Ch1, dc in first 10 sts, (4dc, 2dc in next st) 3 times, dc in last 10 sts, turn. [38 sts]
Row 7 Ch1, dc in first 10 sts, (5dc, 2dc in next st) 3 times, dc in last 10 sts, turn. [41 sts]
Row 8 Ch1, dc in first 10 sts, 2dc, 4htr, 2htr in next st, 6htr, 2htr in next st, 5htr, 1dc, 2dc in next st, dc in last 10 sts, fasten off leaving a long tail.

TOP
With Apple Granny and a 3mm hook, ch22.
Row 1 (RS) Dc in second ch from hook and in each ch to end, turn. [21 sts]
Rows 2-49 Ch1, dc in each st to end, turn.
It's a good idea to work a few more rows than you think you'll need to fit around the long curved edge of the Back. When fitting these two pieces together, you can always undo any extra rows once it's been sewn in position. Fasten off leaving a long tail.

HANDLE
Cut a 12cm piece of gold wired braid with wire cutters and fold the two ends into the centre so that it's folded in half, but with the ends meeting at the centre on one side. Put a blob of glue on the ends of the wire to stop them fraying.
With Chocolate and a 2.5mm hook, ch9.
Row 1 Dc in second ch from hook and in each ch to end, turn. [8 sts]
Row 2 Ch1, dc in each st to end, turn.
Row 3 Ch1, insert the hook into the back loop only of the next st and into the first rem loop of the foundation ch at the same time, before completing a dc stitch. Work in the same way in the rem sts, around the piece of wired braid so that the rows form a tube encasing the braid, fasten off and weave in ends.

  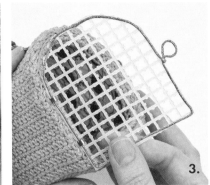

LINING AND DOOR

Use the Base, Back and Top as templates for cutting pieces from the lining fabric. The fabric will need to be slightly smaller than the actual pieces, but you can always trim it to fit later. Use the Back as a template for cutting a piece from the plastic canvas for the door. If you have the patience, cut alternate cross pieces from the canvas with a craft knife to make larger holes!

TO MAKE UP

Split a strand of Apple Granny in half to sew the pieces together, as this makes for a neater seam. First sew the long edge of the Top piece to fit around the sides and curved top of the Back piece. Remove any extra rows of the Top piece. Before sewing on the Base, stick the lining fabric pieces on the inside of the Top and Back with craft glue, trimming to fit if necessary. Sew the short edge of the Base to the remaining edge of the Back piece to make sure it is placed centrally. Sew one long edge of the Base to a short edge of the Top, then stick the lining fabric on the inside of the Base. Sew the remaining side closed and weave in ends.

To reinforce the Front, take 2 pipe cleaners and twist them together, then cut to 25cm long with wire cutters.

With Apple Granny and a 3mm hook, ch56, or a length of chain the same length as the pipe cleaner when stretched slightly. Work 55 dc sts along this chain, then another 2 rows of dc. On the 4th row, enclose the pipe cleaners by working a dc seam along

the length, and inserting the hook into the loop of the next foundation ch and the next st of the previous row at the same time and completing a dc stitch. Fasten off leaving a long tail.

This pipe cleaner length will fit around the inside of the front opening with the ends meeting in the centre at the bottom. Make the first bend in the pipe cleaner length so that the end of the length lies at the centre bottom. Starting in the corner by the bend, whipstitch the outside loop of each dc stitch on the last row to the front edge of the Basket. Work all the way round, bending the length when you reach the second corner. Sew the two ends of the pipe cleaner length together using the finishing tail.

Sew the Top Handle to the centre top with sewing thread {1}. Take the remaining piece of gold wired braid and stick it around the outside edge of the door, creating a loop about 1cm long on the middle of the right-hand side for the fastening. Where the ends of the wire meet, trim them with wire cutters and smooth the ends with craft glue to stop them fraying and make a neat join. Use a paper fastener on the right-hand side to make a door knob {2}. Use the other two paper fasteners on the opposite side as door hinges, inserting them from the inside to the outside behind the pipe cleaner strip so that the 'legs' of the fastener come through to the right side. Bend each leg of the fastener around the outside edge of the door with pliers so that they overlap, trimming to fit with wire cutters {3}.

chapter six: betty's boudoir

No self-respecting fashionista ignores her undergarments, and Betty is just as well dressed in private as she is in public. Her corset gives her the 1950s hourglass figure, and her baby doll bed set makes sure she's at her best when she answers the door to the postman. Bert's curled up for the night in his basket and just in case he sees more than he should do, he's got an eye mask, because let's face it, cats don't need much help sleeping!

Total yarn quantities for this section: Scheepjes Catona 80g of Chrystalline (385), 30g of Soft Rose (409), 5g of Rose Wine (396), 10g of Chocolate (507), 5g of Cyan (397), 25g of Jet Black (110), 15g of Saffron (249), 30cm length of Snow White (106). Check the yarn quantities needed for all projects on page 121.

baby doll pyjamas

The frilly details on the top and bed jacket are a girly delight and the colour co-ordinates exactly with her bedlinen. All she needs now is a cup of tea in her favourite china, and she'll be all set for a lazy Sunday morning

Materials

- ▇ Scheepjes Catona, Chrystalline (30g for Top, 15g for Pants)
- ▇ A 2.5mm hook
- ▇ A 3mm hook
- ▇ Button, 5mm
- ▇ White shirring elastic
- ▇ 25cm of white cord elastic
- ▇ 1m ribbon, 1cm wide
- ▇ Craft glue
- ▇ Sewing thread
- ▇ Yarn needle for cord elastic
- ▇ Stitch marker

Note

There are two sections to the Top; the Bra and the Skirt. Two Cups are made for the Bra, they're sewn together and a round is worked around the outside of the two Cups, which includes the overarm straps. For the Skirt, an extension ch is attached to the left side, and then the yarn is rejoined on the opposite side to work another ch, and the stitches of the Skirt are worked across the ch, the base of the Cups and the extension ch. Shirring elastic is threaded through the stitches underneath the Cups, and a button is attached at the centre back for fastening. The ends of the straps are sewn to the first row of the Skirt at the back.

PYJAMA TOP

Front

Back

Cups (make 2)

Work in a spiral without closing off each round with a ss.

With Chrystalline and a 3mm hook, make a magic loop.

Round 1 (RS) 6dc into loop. [6 sts]

Work in back loops only for the rest of the Cup.

Round 2 (2dc in next st, 1dc) 3 times. [9 sts]

Round 3 (2dc in next st, 1dc) 4 times, 2dc in next st. [14 sts]

Round 4 2dc, (2dc in next st, 2dc) 4 times. [18 sts]

Round 5 (partial round) 2dc, htr in next st, tr in next st, fasten off.

On the second cup, mark the 8th st of Round 4, omit the last tr st on Round 5 and leave a long tail for sewing.

Position the Cups side by side as shown in the Baby Doll Top: Bra Chart on page 131 and sew the last 3 sts of each cup together in the centre.

Rejoin Chrystalline with a ss in the marked st of Round 4 on the second Cup with RS facing. Refer to the Baby Doll Top: Bra Chart on page 131.

Round 1 (RS) Ss in next st, 2dc in next st, htr in next st, tr in next st, 2dc around post of tr just worked, dc in st at base of tr, dc in next 6 sts along base of Cup, 2dc around post of next tr, dc in st at base of tr, dc in next 5 sts along base of first Cup, ch3 (counts as tr), tr in next unworked st of first Cup, htr in next st, dc in next st, 2dc in next st, ss in next st, ch19 for strap, ss in second ch from hook and each ch back towards Cup, ss in st at base of ch. Ss evenly around top of first Cup, into centre and top of second Cup until you have worked a ss in the st before the marked st, ch19 for strap, ss in second ch from hook and each ch back towards Cup, ss in st at base of ch, ss in marked st, fasten off.

SKIRT

Refer to the Baby Doll Top: Skirt Chart on page 131. Make an extension ch for the left side of the Skirt as follows:

With Chrystalline and a 3mm hook, ss to top of ch-3 on first Cup with RS facing, ch10, fasten off.

Rejoin Chrystalline on the opposite side at the base of the second Cup with RS facing, in the first dc worked around the post of the tr.

Row 1 (RS) Ch10, ch4 for button loop, skip the last 4 ch worked, dc in each rem ch back towards Cup, dc in next 17 sts along base of Cups, 3dc in ch-3, dc in each ch of extension ch, turn. [40 sts and ch-4 button loop]. In the (dc, ch1) rib pattern that follows, ch always count as sts.

Row 2 Ch1, *(dc in next st, ch1) twice, skip next st; rep from * to last st, dc in last st, turn. [53 sts]

Row 3 Ch1, (dc, ch1) in each dc across to last dc, dc in last dc, turn. [53 sts]

Row 4 Ch1, (dc, ch1) in each st and ch-sp across to last dc, dc in last dc, turn. [105 sts]

Rows 5-17 Ch1, (dc, ch1) in each dc across to last dc, dc in last dc, turn. [105 sts]

Change to a 2.5mm hook for picot edging:

Row 18 *Ss in next st, ch3, ss in first of those ch, ss in next st, ch1; rep from * to last st, ss in last st, fasten off and weave in ends.

TO MAKE UP

Take a length of white shirring elastic 60cm long and fold it in half. Thread a needle with the two raw ends so that the elastic is doubled. With WS facing, anchor the elastic at one end of Row 1 of the Skirt by inserting the needle into the back of a stitch and then putting the needle through the loop of elastic and pulling it tight. Thread the elastic through the back of the stitches of Row 1, pull up so that the Skirt is gathered slightly and secure at the other end of Row 1. Fasten off.

Sew a button to the opposite end of Row 1 from the button loop, and sew the ends of the straps to the top of Row 1 at the back.

Trimming
Make a picot length to fit across the top of the Skirt with Chrystalline and a 2.5mm hook:
(Ch3, ss in first of those ch, ch1) repeat until the length will fit across the first ch, underneath the Cups and across the second ch at the top of the Skirt. Fasten off, leaving a tail to sew this in position, using the image as a guide. Weave in ends.

Sew a running stitch along the centre of the ribbon with sewing thread, and pull up so that the ribbon ruffles. Continue until the ruffle will fit around the top edge of the Cups, with a V-shaped indent in the centre. Secure the running thread once the ruffle is the right length. Sew the ruffle in position, cutting the ribbon to length and sealing the ends with a little craft glue to stop fraying.

PANTS
These are worked from side to side, with the foundation ch and last row forming the centre seam. In the (dc, ch1) rib pattern beg in Row 1, ch always count as sts.

Right and Left side (make 2)
With Chrystalline and a 3mm hook, ch18, leaving a long tail at the beg of the ch for sewing up later.
Row 1 (RS) Dc in second ch from hook, ch1, skip next ch, (dc in next ch, ch1, skip next ch) repeat to last ch, dc in last ch, turn. [17 sts]
Rows 2-22 Ch1, (dc in next dc, ch1, skip next ch) repeat to last st, dc in last st, turn, do not fasten off.

Gusset
Row 23 Ch1, dc in next 2 sts, turn leaving rem sts unworked. [2 sts]

Front

Back

Rows 24-32 Ch1, 2dc, turn.
Fasten off leaving a long tail for sewing up.

TO MAKE UP
Refer to Baby Doll Pants Diagram on page 132.

Folding the Gusset piece around to form a tube, sew the last 2 sts of the Gusset to the first 2 sts of the foundation ch. Repeat for the second piece, and using the remaining thread, align the two Gusset pieces RS together and sew together along the top edge.

Decide which is to be the Back, and sew the last row of one piece to the foundation row of the other piece for 4 sts from the bottom, leaving the remaining sts left unsewn so that there's a gap in the centre back seam for putting the Pants on Betty.

Using the long starting tail at the front, sew the last row and first row together down the centre front, weave in all ends.

Using cord elastic and a large-eyed yarn needle, thread the elastic through the back of the sts on the WS at the waist. Draw up the elastic and arrange so that the ends emerge on one side of the gap. Tie the ends together, thread each end back through the stitches and trim so that the ends are held in place by a few stitches on each side.

Thread a needle with a double length of shirring elastic and secure on the WS leg edge as for the instructions on the Baby Doll Top. Thread the elastic through the sts just inside the edge of the leg, pulling up to gather, secure firmly. Repeat for other leg.

BED JACKET
Materials
▨ Scheepjes Catona, Chrystalline (35g)

▨ A 2.5mm hook

▨ A 3mm hook

▨ 1m ribbon, 1cm wide (to match that used on the Baby Doll Pyjamas)

▨ White shirring elastic

▨ Stitch markers

Note
The Bed Jacket is worked with a top down Yoke, then rotated to work side to side, slip stitching the end of each row into the next st of the last row of the Yoke.

YOKE
With Chrystalline and a 3mm hook, ch37.
Row 1 (RS) Dc in second ch from hook and in each ch to end, turn. [36 sts]
Row 2 Ch1, dc in first 2 sts, (2dc in next st, 5dc) 5 times, 2dc in next st, dc in last 3 sts, turn. [42 sts]

Row 3 Ch1, dc in each st to end, turn.
Row 4 Ch1, (6dc, 2dc in next st) 6 times, turn. [48 sts]
Row 5 Ch1, dc in each st to end, turn.
Row 6 Ch1, dc in first 3 sts, (2dc in next st, 7dc) 5 times, 2dc in next st, dc in last 4 sts, turn, do not fasten off. [54 sts]

BODY
Refer to the Bed Jacket: Body Chart and Bed Jacket: Sleeve Chart on page 133.
The Body Chart shows the last row of the Yoke, and the Body rows worked into each st of the Yoke.
With Chrystalline and a 3mm hook, ch23. The row worked into this ch will form the Left Front edge of the Jacket. Place markers in the 9th and 20th dc sts from the ch (first and last sts of first Sleeve), and in the 36th and 47th dc sts from the ch (first and last sts of second Sleeve).

Left Front
Row 1 (RS) Dc in second ch from hook and in each ch back towards Yoke, ss in st at base of ch. [22 dc and 1 ss]
Row 2 Ss in next unworked st of Yoke, turn, working in front loops only; skip 2 ss, 7dc, 7htr, 8tr, turn. [22 sts and 1 ss]
Row 3 Ch1, working in front loops only; 22dc, ss in next unworked st of Yoke. [22dc and 1 ss]
Rows 4-7 Repeat Rows 2 and 3 twice more.
Row 8 Repeat Row 2.

The next unworked st of the Yoke will be the first marked st of the Sleeve. The following rows will form the Body and will not be joined to the Yoke, leaving the marked sts and those between them for working the Sleeve later:
Row 9 Ch1, working in front loops only; 22dc, turn. [22 dc]
Row 10 Ch1, working in front loops only; 7dc, 7htr, 8tr, turn.

Front

Back

Rows 11-14 Repeat Rows 9-10 twice more.

Back

Now continue joining to the sts of the Yoke as before. The ss at the end of Row 15 will be worked into the st after the second marked st, skipping the sts for the Sleeve:

Row 15 As Row 3.

Rows 16-29 As Rows 2 and 3 seven more times.

The next unworked st of the Yoke should be the third marked st. Do not join the following rows to the Yoke as before:

Row 30 As Row 10.

Rows 31-36 Repeat Rows 9 and 10 three more times.

Right Front

Continue joining to the sts of the Yoke as before. The ss at the end of Row 37 will be worked into the st after the fourth marked st, skipping the sts for the Sleeve:

Row 37 As Row 3.

Rows 38-43 Repeat Rows 2 and 3 three more times. Fasten off.

SLEEVES

Rejoin Chrystalline to the first marked st with RS facing, ch 13.

Row 1 (RS) Dc in second ch from hook and in each ch back towards Yoke, ss in st at base of ch. [12 sts]

Row 2 Ss in next unworked st of Yoke, turn, skip 2 ss, working in front loops only; 12dc, turn.

Row 3 Ch1, working in front loops only; 12dc, ss in next unworked st of Yoke. [12 dc, 1 ss]

Rows 4-11 Repeat Rows 2 and 3 four more times.

Row 12 Repeat Row 2. The ss this row should be worked into the next marked st.

Do not join the following rows to the Yoke:

Rows 13-18 Ch1, working in front loops only; 12dc, turn. Fasten off leaving a long tail.

Fold the unattached portion of the Sleeve round into a tube and sew the first row to the last row using the long tail. Thread the yarn through to the WS, and holding the two open edges together, sew together the underarms from the WS.

Repeat for the second Sleeve, rejoining the yarn to the third marker.

Cuffs

Turn the Jacket WS out.

Thread a needle with a double length of shirring elastic and secure as for the instructions on the Baby Doll Top, on the WS Cuff edge. Thread the elastic through the sts just inside the edge of the Cuff, pulling up slightly to gather and secure firmly. Repeat for other Cuff.

Picot Edging and Trimming

Rejoin Chrystalline to the hem edge with RS facing, and with a 2.5mm hook.

Ch3, ss in first of those ch (ch-3 picot made), *ss in next tr row end, ch1, ss in same tr row end, ch-3 picot, ss in next dc row end, ch1, ss in next tr row end, ch-3 picot, ss in same tr row end, ch1, ss in next dc row end, ch-3 picot; rep from * around the hem edge. Fasten off and weave in ends.

Continuing with a 2.5mm hook and Chrystalline, make a picot length to fit across the bottom of the Yoke as follows:

(Ch-3 picot, ch1) repeat until the length will fit around Row 6 of the Yoke, fasten off leaving a long tail and use the tail to sew the length into position.

HAIR WITH CURLERS
Materials
▨ Scheepjes Catona, Chocolate (10g)

▨ A 3mm hook

▨ Silicone drinking straws

▨ Craft glue

▨ Craft knife and cutting mat

▨ Black shirring elastic and hook and loop fastening if making the Hair removable

▨ Dressmaking pins

Note
The Hair Cap is made first and then pieces of the drinking straw are wrapped with yarn and glued to the Hair Cap.

HAIR CAP
The main part of the Hair Cap is worked in the back loops only throughout. Make the first ear piece before continuing to the Hair Cap:

With Chocolate and a 3mm hook, ch5, leaving a long starting tail.

Ss in second ch from hook and next ch, dc in next ch, htr in next ch, do not fasten off.

Ch18.

Row 1 (RS) Htr in second ch from hook and next ch, 4dc, 5ss, 4dc, 2htr, turn. [17 sts]

Row 2 Ch1 (does not count as st throughout), working in back loops only; 2htr in first st, htr in next st, 4dc, 5ss, 4dc, htr in next st, 2htr in last st, turn. [19 sts]

Row 3 Ch1, 3htr, 4dc, 5ss, 5dc, htr in next st, 2htr in last st, turn. [20 sts]

Row 4 Ch1, 2htr in first st, htr in next st, 6dc, 5ss, 5dc, htr in next st, 2htr in last st, turn. [22 sts]

Row 5 Ch1, 3htr, 5dc, 5ss, 7dc, htr in next st, 2htr in last st, turn. [23 sts]

Row 6 Ch1, 2htr in first st, htr in next st, 8dc, 5ss, 6dc, htr in next st, 2htr in last st, turn. [25 sts]

Row 7 Ch1, 3htr, 6dc, 5ss, 8dc, 3htr, turn.

Row 8 Ch1, htr2tog, htr in next st, 8dc, 5ss, 6dc, htr

in next st, htr2tog, turn. [23 sts]

Row 9 Ch1, 3htr, 5dc, 5ss, 7dc, htr in next st, htr2tog, turn. [22 sts]

Row 10 Ch1, htr2tog, htr in next st, 6dc, 5ss, 5dc, htr in next st, htr2tog, turn. [20 sts]

Row 11 Ch1, 3htr, 4dc, 5ss, 5dc, htr in next st, htr2tog, turn. [19 sts]

Row 12 Ch1, htr2tog, htr in next st, 4dc, 5ss, 4dc, htr in next st, htr2tog, turn. [17 sts]

Row 13 Ch1, 2htr, 4dc, 5ss, 4dc, 2htr, do not fasten off.

For second ear piece, ch5, ss in second ch from hook and next ch, dc in next ch, htr in next ch, ss in edge of Hair Cap, fasten off leaving a long tail. Refer to Hair with Curlers Diagram on page 132.

Use the tail to sew the first half of the last row to the second half of the last row. Use the starting tail to sew the htr of the first ear piece to the edge of the Cap, then sew the first half of the foundation ch to the second half of the foundation ch.

Weave in ends. Sew the Hair Cap to the head, or if you're making the hair removable, run a doubled length of black shirring elastic inside the edge of the Hair Cap, pulling it up slightly before securing the end. Stick or sew a piece of hook and loop fastening inside the Cap.

CURLERS

Cut each drinking straw into sections approx 13mm long. The exact length doesn't matter, but keep them all the same size, and you'll need about 34 pieces in total. You can mark the length with a piece of masking tape on your cutting mat to use as a guide for keeping them the same length.

Put a little craft glue on each piece, and wind Chocolate yarn evenly around, putting the beginning and end of the yarn on the same side of the curler so that it can be hidden by sticking it to the Hair Cap on this side. Leave to dry, then position the curlers on the Hair Cap. It's easiest to do this by putting the Cap on the Head and pinning them in position. Once you're happy with the placement you can glue each one in place.

STRING OF PEARLS
Materials
▪ Small pearl beads (as many as it takes to thread a length of 8cm)

▪ 20cm nylon beading thread

▪ Small magnetic jewellery clasp

Thread the beads onto the beading thread. Pass the end of the thread through the clasp and back down through a few of the beads, tie off the end and trim. Repeat for the other end of the thread.

betty's corseterie

A corset isn't the most comfortable garment Betty has ever worn, but it's essential to maintaining her slender 1950s waistline. That criss-cross elastic holds her tummy in place, and the eye mask and slippers complete the set

Materials

- Scheepjes Catona, Soft Rose (20g)
- Scheepjes Catona, Rose Wine (5g)
- A 3mm hook
- 30cm ribbon, 4mm wide
- 40cm pink cord elastic
- 4 square jump rings (from a jewellery supplier)
- 2 press fasteners
- Sewing thread
- Craft glue

See note about decreasing on page 10.

Note

The Corset is worked from the bottom up in one piece, with an overlap on one side so that you can remove it. The yarn is rejoined at the bottom and a round is worked to join the overlap stitches together. A gusset strip is worked from the last round and sewn to the opposite side.

CORSET

Front

With Soft Rose and a 3mm hook, ch41.

Row 1 (WS) Dc in second ch from hook and in each ch to end, turn. [40 sts]

Rows 2-8 Ch1, dc in each st to end, turn.

Row 9 Ch1, dec, dc in each st to last 2 sts, dec, turn. [38 sts]

Row 10 Ch1, dc in each st to end, turn.

Row 11 Ch1, (11dc, dec) twice, 12dc, turn. [36 sts]

Row 12 Ch1, 5dc, dec, 22dc, dec, 5dc, turn. [34 sts]

Row 13 Ch1, 9dc, dec, 12dc, dec, 9dc, turn. [32 sts]

Row 14 Ch1, 5dc, dec, 18dc, dec, 5dc, turn. [30 sts]

Row 15 Ch1, dc in each st to end, turn.

Row 16 Ch1, 8dc, 2dc in next st, 4dc, 2dc in next st, 8dc, 2dc in next st, 4dc, 2dc in next st, 2dc, turn. [34 sts]

Rows 17-19 Ch1, dc in each st to end, turn.

Back

Row 20 Ch1, (6dc, 2dc in next st) 4 times, 6dc, turn. [38 sts]

Row 21 Ch1, 5dc, (2dc in next st, 7dc) 4 times, 1dc, turn. [42 sts]

Row 22 Ch1, dc in each st to end, turn.

Row 23 Ch1, (8dc, 2dc in next st) 4 times, 6dc, turn. [46 sts]

Row 24 Ch1, dc in each st to end, turn, do not fasten off.

Cups

See the Corset Cups Chart on page 131.

Row 25 (WS) Ch1, dc in each st to last 13 sts, 1htr, 2tr in next st, 1htr, 4dc, 1htr, 2tr in next st, 1htr, 3dc, turn. [48 sts]

Row 26 (RS) Ch1, *2dc, 2htr, 2tr in next st, 1tr, 2htr; rep from * once more, dc in next st, 1ss, turn leaving rem sts unworked. [20 sts including ss]

Row 27 Skip ss, ss in next dc, *1dc, 2htr, 2htr in next st, 2htr, dc in next st, ss in next 2 sts; rep from * once more, turn. [21 sts including ss]

Row 28 Skip ss, dc in next ss, 2htr, 1tr, 2tr in next st, 1tr, 1htr, 1dc, 4ss, 1dc, 1htr, 1tr, 2tr in next st, 1tr, 2htr, 1dc, ss in base of st at end of Row 26, turn. [23 sts including ss]

Row 29 Skip first ss, ss in each st to end, skipping centre 2 ss, fasten off.

With the Cup side of the Corset on top, overlap the first and last 2 sts of Row 1 and tack in position. Rejoin Soft Rose with the RS facing in the remaining loop of the foundation ch at the centre back, dc in each st around, working through both layers when you get to the overlapped stitches, ss to first dc to join, turn. Work another round of dc working in the back loops only of each stitch, fasten off.

Gusset

You'll rejoin Soft Rose in the remaining front loops of the previous round to work the Gusset, so flatten the Corset and mark the central back 4 sts. Rejoin the yarn in the first of these sts with RS facing.

Row 1 (RS) Ch1, dc in front loops of 4 central sts, turn. [4 sts]

Row 2 Ch1, dec, 2dc, turn. [3 sts]

Row 3 Ch1, dec, 1dc, turn. [2 sts]

Rows 4-6 Ch1, dc in each st, turn.

Row 7 Ch1, 2dc in first st, dc in last st, turn. [3 sts]

Row 8 Ch1, 2dc in first st, 2dc, fasten off leaving a long tail.

Use the tail of yarn to sew the other side of the Gusset to the opposite 4 sts. Weave in ends.

TO FINISH

With Rose Wine and a 3mm hook work a round of slip stitch surface crochet between Rows 15 and 16 at the waist. Repeat underneath the Cups between Rows 24 and 25. With Rose Wine, embroider a back stitch along the overlap edge, along Row 27 of the Cups and down the front on the other side to mirror the shape along the overlap edge, fasten off. Thread another piece of yarn through the back stitches, taking the needle from top to bottom through each stitch like a whipstitch. This will help to correct any unevenness in the stitching lines.

Cut a piece of pink ribbon 5cm long and fold in half, slipping a jump ring over the fold. Sew the ends inside the bottom edge in line with the line of stitching. Put a little craft glue between the ribbon near the fold to hold the jump ring in place. Repeat for the other side at the front and opposite at the back – a total of 4 pieces.

CORSET 'LACING'

Find the centre of the piece of cord elastic and sew it with thread for a few stitches on each side, about 4 stitches apart under the waistline, using the image as a guide. Cross over the ends of elastic and sew each piece in line with the previous stitching 4 rows below. Continue until you reach the bottom, then pass the ends of the elastic through to the inside of the Corset.

Secure with a few stitches and a little craft glue on the ends to stop fraying.

Sew a press fastener underneath the overlap at the waist and one at the top corner of the Cups.

HAIR RIBBON

Materials

▪ 20cm pink ribbon, 4mm wide

▪ 25cm pink cord elastic

▪ Sewing thread

Tie a bow with the ribbon and sew a few stitches in the back to hold it in place. Measure the cord elastic around the Bun from the Hair in a Bun piece and overlap the ends slightly. Cut and sew through the overlapped ends. Before fastening off sew the ribbon over the join.

EYE MASK
Materials
■ Scheepjes Catona, Soft Rose (5g)

■ A 3mm hook

■ White braid

■ White shirring elastic

■ Lining fabric (see note on page 11)

■ Craft glue

With Soft Rose and a 3mm hook, ch11.
Round 1 (RS) Dc in second ch from hook and next 8 ch, 3dc in next ch, rotate to work in other side of foundation ch, dc in next 8 ch, 2dc in last ch, ss to first st to join. [22 sts]
Round 2 Ch1, 2dc in first st, 8dc, 2dc in next 2 sts, (dc, htr) in next st, 2tr, htr in next st, dc in next st, ss in sp before next st, dc in next st, htr in next st, 2tr, (htr, dc) in next st, 2dc in next st, ss to first st, ch35 for strap, ss in second ch from hook and in each ch back to Mask, fasten off and weave in ends. Sew other end of strap to opposite side of Mask.

Use the Mask as a template to draw around on the lining fabric, cutting inside the line to make a smaller piece. Stick the fabric to the WS of the Mask using craft glue. Run a doubled length of shirring elastic inside the strap and pull up slightly before securing. Stick white braid around the outside edge of the Mask as decoration.

SLIPPERS
Materials
■ Scheepjes Catona, Soft Rose (5g)

■ A 2.5mm hook

■ White braid for decoration

■ Toy stuffing

■ Craft glue

Note
Each pair of Slippers is made from two Soles joined together with a crocheted seam.

SOLE
With Soft Rose and a 2.5mm hook, ch11.
Starting at the heel:
Round 1 (RS) Htr in third ch from hook (skipped ch count as st), dc in next 5 ch, htr in next ch, tr in next ch, (tr, 4htr, tr) in next ch, rotate to work in other side of foundation ch, tr in next ch, htr in next ch, dc in next 5 ch, (2htr, 4tr) in next ch, ss to top of beg ch-2. [28 sts] Fasten off first Sole, then make another without fastening off.

With Soles WS together, and working through the outside loop only of both layers, crochet the two Soles together as follows, putting a small amount of toy stuffing into the heel end before completing the following round: Htr in first 2 sts, 2dc, 14ss, 2dc, 6htr, ss to first st, fasten off.

FRONT BAND

With Soft Rose, ch7 leaving a long starting tail.

Row 1 Dc in second ch from hook and in each ch to end, turn. [6 sts]
Row 2 Ch1, dc in each st to end, fasten off leaving a long tail.
Use the tails of yarn to sew the Band to the front of the Slipper.
Stick a small piece of white braid to the Front Band with craft glue and weave in all ends.

CURLED-UP BERT
Materials
- Scheepjes Catona, Jet Black (25g)
- A 30cm length of Scheepjes Catona, Soft Rose
- A 30cm length of Scheepjes Catona, Snow White
- A 2.5mm hook
- Plastic toy filling granules
- Old black tights
- Craft glue

See note about decreasing on page 10.

Measurements
Bert measures 7x8cm, and 3cm tall.

NECK AND TOP BODY

With Jet Black and a 2.5mm hook, ch10 leaving a long starting tail, ss to first ch, being careful not to twist. Work in a spiral in front loops only unless stated otherwise.
Round 1 (RS) Ch1, dc in each ch around. [10 sts]
Rounds 2-3 Dc in each st around.
Round 4 2dc in first st, dc in each rem st around. [11 sts]
Round 5 As Round 4. [12 sts]
Round 6 (2dc in next st, dc in next st) 6 times. [18 sts]
Round 7 Dc in each st around.
Round 8 4dc, 2dc in next st, 8dc, 2dc in next st,

4dc. [20 sts]
Round 9 Dc in each st around.
Round 10 5dc, 2dc in next st, 8dc, 2dc in next st, 5dc. [22 sts]
Do not fasten off.

Body
Round 1 (RS) Ch1, 5dc, (2dc in next st) twice, 8dc, (2dc in next st) twice, 5dc. [26 sts]
Round 2 4dc, 2dc in next st, 16dc, 2dc in next st, 4dc. [28 sts]
Rounds 3-4 Dc in each st around.
Round 5 5dc, 2dc in next st, 16dc, 2dc in next st, 5dc. [30 sts]
Rounds 6-7 Dc in each st around.
Round 8 9dc, (2dc in next st) twice, 8dc, (2dc in next st) twice, 9dc. [34 sts]
Round 9 Dc in each st around.
Round 10 2dc, dec, 1dc, dec, 20dc, dec, 1dc, dec, 2dc. [30 sts]

Round 11 (2dc, dec) 3 times, 6dc, (dec, 2dc) 3 times. [24 sts]

Round 12 (1dc, dec) 3 times, 6dc, (dec, 1dc) 3 times. [18 sts]

Round 13 (1dc, dec) 3 times, (dec, 1dc) 3 times, do not fasten off. [12 sts]

Using the starting tail, run a gathering thread around the Neck, pull tight and secure to close leaving a long tail. Fill the Body with plastic granules, but do not stuff all the way into the narrow part of the Neck.

Round 14 (Dec) 6 times, fasten off. [6 sts]

Tail

With Jet Black and a 2.5mm hook, ch15.

Row 1 Dc in second ch from hook and in each ch to end, turn. [14 sts]

Row 2 Ch1, working in both loops, dc in each st to last st, ss in last st, turn. [13 sts, 1ss]

Row 3 Skip ss, dc in each rem st to end, fasten off leaving a long tail.

Use the tail end of yarn to sew to the fasten off point of the Body, sewing a few extra sts between the start of the tail and the Body to make it curl around the front of the Body.

Weave in ends.

Head

Work the Head and Face Details as for Sitting-up Bert on page 39. The Head pattern has a ch-3 sp in Round 7 which is used in other versions of Bert as a hole for the Neck. The Neck will not be joined here in this version, but it's easier to leave it in and use it for stuffing the Head, as it will be hidden once you've sewn the Head to the Body.

TO MAKE UP

Curl the Neck piece round to the front of the Body and sew in position. Sew the Head to the Body, covering the join of the Neck.

BERT'S BASKET

Materials

◾ Scheepjes Catona, Saffron (15g)

◾ A 3mm hook

◾ 2 pipe cleaners, 30cm long

◾ Wire cutters

◾ Lining fabric and craft glue
   (optional, see note on page 11)

With Saffron and a 3mm hook, ch9.

Round 1 (RS) Dc in second ch from hook and next

6 ch, 3dc in next ch, rotate to work in other side of foundation ch, dc in next 6 sts, 2dc in last st, ss to first dc to join. [18 sts]

Round 2 Ch1, 2dc in first st, 6dc, 2dc in next 3 sts, 6dc, 2dc in last 2 sts, ss to first dc. [24 sts]

Round 3 Ch1, dc in next st, 2dc in next st, 6dc, (dc in next st, 2dc in next st) 3 times, 6dc, (dc in next st, 2dc in next st) twice, ss to first dc. [30 sts]

Round 4 Ch1, 2dc, 2dc in next st, 6dc, (2dc, 2dc in next st) 3 times, 6dc, (2dc, 2dc in next st) twice, ss to first dc. [36 sts]

Round 5 Ch1, 3dc, 2dc in next st, 6dc, (3dc, 2dc in next st) 3 times, 6dc, (3dc, 2dc in next st) twice, ss to first dc. [42 sts]

Round 6 Ch1, 4dc, 2dc in next st, 6dc, (4dc, 2dc in next st) 3 times, 6dc, (4dc, 2dc in next st) twice, ss to first dc. [48 sts]

Round 7 Ch1, 5dc, 2dc in next st, 6dc, (5dc, 2dc in next st) 3 times, 6dc, (5dc, 2dc in next st) twice, ss to first dc. [54 sts]

Round 8 Working in back loops only, dc in each st around, do not close round with a ss but continue working in a spiral with a dc in next 7 sts to bring you to the new start to work back and forth in rows, turn.

Row 9 (WS) Ch1, dc in each st around to last 6 sts, turn leaving rem sts unworked. [48 sts]

Row 10 Ch1, dc2tog, dc in each st around to last 2 sts, dc2tog, turn. [46 sts]

Row 11 As Row 10. [44 sts]

Rows 12-15 Ch1, dc in each st to end, turn.

Row 16 Ch1, dc in each st to end, ss into last 4 row ends, dc in next 2 row ends, dc2tog over next row end and first of 6 skipped sts at base of opening, dc in next 4 sts, dc2tog over next st and next row end, dc in next 2 row ends, fasten off leaving a long tail.

Twist the two pipe cleaners together to make a doubled length. Fold the last 4 rows to the outside of the Basket and use to enclose the pipe cleaners. Sew all round using the tail of yarn and trim the ends of the

pipe cleaners with wire cutters to fit. Fasten off and weave in ends.

The base of the Basket may not lie very flat, in which case spray it with some spray starch, pin out the base section on a flat surface and leave to dry. If lining the Basket, draw round the base of the Basket on the reverse of the pre-prepared lining fabric, check the fit and trim, then stick in place.

BERT'S EYE MASK
Materials
▪ Scheepjes Catona, Cyan (5g)
▪ A 2.5mm hook
▪ Black shirring elastic
▪ Lining fabric (see note on page 11)
▪ Craft glue

Using a 2.5mm hook, follow instructions for Eye Mask for Betty on page 90. Do not make the strap, and do not add any decoration. Use a doubled piece of black shirring elastic as the strap on the Mask, and this can sit around Bert's ears.

chapter seven: betty goes dancing

Betty is armed with her handbag and dancing shoes and is ready to swing. Ever-prepared, she's got her frilly underskirt to keep her skirt in place when she's not twirling. All that dancing is a bit much for Bert. He prefers to tune in on the wireless at home and tap his paw to the music when he thinks no-one is looking

Total yarn quantities for this section: Scheepjes Catona 45g of Lemonade (403), 30g of Candy Apple (516), 10g of Cyan (397), 50g of Snow White (106), 5g of Chocolate (507), 60cm length of Jet Black (110) **Scheepjes Maxi Sweet Treat** 5g of Lemonade (403). Check the yarn quantities needed for all projects on page 121.

betty's rockabilly dress

Betty's delicious lemon yellow dancing dress catches the eye of a few would-be partners on the dance floor. She's ready for some jiving with her full skirt and petticoat. The red trim, sash and buttons make the yellow come alive

Materials

- Scheepjes Catona, Lemonade (40g)
- Scheepjes Catona, Candy Apple (10g)
- Scheepjes Maxi Sweet Treat, Lemonade (5g) (See Note below)
- A 2.5mm hook
- A 3mm hook
- 5 buttons, 5mm

Note

Worked from the waist down, and then the waist up. The top of the Skirt is made using Scheepjes Maxi to reduce the bulk of the gathered fabric at the waist, and then it's used for one row out of every four to create a lacy effect. If you prefer not to work with a finer yarn, then make the Skirt as for the Dress on page 30, and work the Body as given below, substituting a row of dc for the Maxi rows. The yarn references in the pattern are to the Catona yarn unless stated otherwise, and Lemonade is used for all except the edging and the Sash.

DANCING DRESS

Front

Back

SKIRT

With Lemonade and a 3mm hook, ch26.
Row 1 (RS) Dc in second ch from hook and in each ch to end, turn, fasten off. [25 sts]
Change to Maxi and a 2.5mm hook.
Row 2 Ch3 (counts as tr throughout), 2tr in same st, 3tr in each rem st to end, turn. [75 sts]
Rows 3-5 Ch3, tr in each st to end, turn.
Fasten off. Change to Catona and continue with a 2.5mm hook.
Row 6 Ch3, tr in each st to end, turn.
Change to a 3mm hook.
Row 7 Ch3, tr in each st to end, turn, fasten off. Change to Maxi and continue with a 3mm hook from here until the hem of the Skirt.
Row 8 Ch2 (counts as htr throughout), htr in each st to end, fasten off. Change to Catona.
Rows 9-10 Ch1, dc in each st to end, turn.
Row 11 Ch1, 2dc, (2dc in next st, 4dc) repeat to last 3 sts, 2dc in next st, 2dc, turn, fasten off. [90 sts]
Row 12 Change to Maxi and repeat Row 8, fasten off. Change to Catona.
Rows 13-15 Ch1, dc in each st to end, turn. Fasten off.
Row 16 Change to Maxi and repeat Row 8, fasten off. Change to Catona.
Rows 17-18 Ch1, dc in each st to end, turn.
Row 19 Ch1, 5dc, (2dc in next st, 9dc) repeat to last 5 sts, 2dc in next st, 4dc, turn, fasten off. [100 sts]
Row 20 Change to Maxi and repeat Row 8, fasten off. Change to Catona.
Rows 21-24 Repeat Rows 13-16.
Fasten off leaving a long tail.
Use the tail of yarn to sew the back seam of the Skirt together, leaving the top 8 rows open.

Edging

Join Candy Apple at the centre back, ch1, dc in each st around, ss to first dc, fasten off and weave in ends.

BODY

Rejoin Lemonade with RS facing in the first st of the other side of the foundation chain. Use a 3mm hook.
Row 1 (RS) Ch1, dc in each ch to end, turn. [25 sts]
Row 2 Ch1, 4dc, 2dc in next st, 3dc, 2dc in next st, 7dc, 2dc in next st, 3dc, 2dc in next st, 4dc, turn. [29 sts]
Row 3 Ch1, (4dc, 2dc in next st) twice, 9dc, (2dc in next st, 4dc) twice, turn. [33 sts]
Row 4 Ch1, (5dc, 2dc in next st) twice, 9dc, (2dc in next st, 5dc) twice, turn. [37 sts]
Row 5 Ch1, 6dc, 2dc in next st, 5dc, 2dc in next st, 11dc, 2dc in next st, 5dc, 2dc in next st, 6dc, turn. [41 sts]
Row 6 Ch1, 10dc, 2dc in next st, 19dc, 2dc in next st, 10dc, turn, fasten off. [43 sts]
Change to Maxi.
Row 7 Ch2, htr in each st to end, turn.
Change to Catona.
Rows 8-10 Ch1, dc in each st to end, turn, fasten off.
Row 11 Change to Maxi and repeat Row 7, turn, fasten off.
Change to Catona.
Row 12 Ch1, dc in each st to end, turn, do not fasten off.

ARMHOLES

See Armhole Chart on page 134.

Row 13 (RS) Ch1, 9dc, ch8 for armhole, skip 4 dc, 17dc, ch8 for armhole, skip 4 dc, 9dc, fasten off. [35 dc and 2 ch-8 sps for Armholes]

Rejoin Lemonade with a ss and RS facing in the third dc to the right of one of the ch-8 sps.
Row 1 (RS) Dc in next 2 sts, dc in each of 8 ch, dc in next 2 sts, ss in next st, turn. [12 dc]
Row 2 Skip ss, dc2tog, 8dc, dc2tog, dc in same st as joining ss, ss in next unworked st, turn. [11 dc]
Row 3 Skip ss, dc in first dc, dc2tog, 6dc, dc2tog,

dc in same st as ss at end of Row 1, ss in next unworked st, turn. [10 dc]

Row 4 Skip ss, dc in first dc, dc2tog, 4dc, dc2tog, dc in next st, dc in same st as ss at end of Row 2, ss in next unworked st, turn. [9 dc]

Row 5 Skip ss, dc in next 2 dc, dc2tog, 2dc, dc2tog, dc in next st, dc in same st as ss at end of Row 3, ss in next unworked st, fasten off.

Rejoin Lemonade in third dc to the right of next ch-8 sp and repeat Rows 1-5 for the other Armhole. Weave in ends.

BUTTONHOLES

Rejoin Lemonade at the bottom of the left side of the back opening. Dc evenly into the row ends until you reach Row 1 of the Skirt. (Ch1, skip next row end, dc in next 2 row ends) 4 times, ch1, skip next row end, dc in last row end, fasten off. The ch-sps in this row form the buttonholes. Sew buttons to the right edge to match buttonholes.

EDGING

Join Candy Apple to the top back neckline opening. Dc evenly around neckline, with a dc2tog at each point where the Armhole joins the Body, fasten off and weave in ends. Join Candy Apple to the first skipped st at the underarm with a ss. Dc in the other side of each Armhole ch, ss in next underarm st, fasten off and weave in ends. Repeat this for the other Armhole.

CRINOLINE UNDERSKIRT
Materials
■ Scheepjes Catona, Snow White (45g)

■ Scheepjes Catona, Candy Apple (5g)

■ A 3mm hook

■ 20cm of white cord elastic

■ Craft glue

Note
The Underskirt is worked from the top down in rows and then joined into the round part way down.

With Snow White and a 3mm hook, ch31.

Row 1 (RS) Dc in second ch from hook, dc in next 4 ch, 2dc in next ch, (dc in next 9ch, 2dc in next ch) twice, dc in last 4 ch, turn. [33 sts]

Row 2 Ch1, 5dc, 2dc in next st, (10dc, 2dc in next st) twice, 5dc, turn. [36 sts]

Row 3 Ch1, 5dc, 2dc in next st, (11dc, 2dc in next st) twice, 6dc, turn. [39 sts]

Row 4 Ch1, 6dc, 2dc in next st, (12dc, 2dc in next st) twice, 6dc, turn. [42 sts]

Row 5 Ch1, dc in each st to end, turn.

Row 6 Ch3 (counts as first tr throughout), tr in each st to last st, 2tr in last st, turn. [43 sts]

Row 7 Ch3, tr in each st to last st, 2tr in last st, ss to top of beg ch-3 to join into the round. [44 sts]

Round 8 (RS) Ch3, tr in same st, tr in each st around, ss to top of beg ch-3. [45 sts]

Round 9 Ch3, tr in each st to last st, 2tr in last st, ss to top of beg ch-3. [46 sts]

Round 10 Ch3, tr in same st, tr in each st around, ss to top of beg ch-3. [47 sts]

Round 11 Working in back loops only, ch3, tr in each st to last st, 2tr in last st, ss to top of beg ch-3, do not fasten off. [48 sts]

First Frill

Round 12 (RS) Ch3, 2tr in same st, 3tr in each st around, ss to top of beg ch-3. [144 sts]

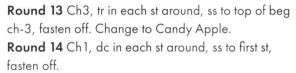

Front

Back

Round 13 Ch3, tr in each st around, ss to top of beg ch-3, fasten off. Change to Candy Apple.
Round 14 Ch1, dc in each st around, ss to first st, fasten off.

Second Frill
Rejoin Snow White in the remaining front loop of Round 10 at the centre back.
Round 1 (RS) Ch3, 2tr in next st, (2tr, 2tr in next st) around, ss to top of beg ch-3. [63 sts]
Round 2 Ch3, 2tr in same st, 3tr in each st around, ss to top of beg ch-3. [189 sts]
Round 3 Ch3, tr in each st around, ss to top of beg ch-3, fasten off.
Change to Candy Apple.
Round 4 Ch1, dc in each st around, ss to first st, fasten off.

Waistband
Rejoin Snow White to first st of other side of foundation ch with RS facing.
Row 1 (RS) Ch1, working over the cord elastic to enclose it, dc in each st on other side of foundation ch to end, fasten off and weave in ends.

Tying off elastic
To hide the knot in the elastic, re-position the ends of the elastic as follows: thread one of the ends of elastic

onto a yarn needle and pass it through a few stitches on the WS on the opposite side of the gap, bringing it out on the WS. Pull out the other end of elastic so that it emerges at the same point. Tie a knot in the elastic so that the gap closes when the elastic is relaxed. Check at this point that the elastic will stretch enough to fit over the Body, then thread each end of elastic back through a few stitches and trim, sealing the ends of the elastic with a little craft glue.

RED BEAD NECKLACE
Materials
- 17 Red wooden beads, 4mm (or as many as it takes to thread a length of 8cm)
- 20cm nylon beading thread
- Small magnetic jewellery clasp

Thread the beads onto the beading thread. Pass the end of the thread through the clasp and back down through a few of the beads, tie off the end and trim. Repeat for the other end of the thread.

HAIR FLOWERS

Materials
- Scheepjes Catona, Lemonade (5g)
- Scheepjes Catona, Chocolate (5g)
- A 3mm hook

Large Flower
With Lemonade and a 3mm hook, ch13 leaving a long starting tail.
Row 1 Dc in second ch from hook and in each ch to end, turn. [12 sts]
Row 2 (Ch1, dc, ch1, ss) in first st, (ss, ch2, htr, ch2, ss) in next 3 sts, (ss, ch3, tr, ch3, ss) in next 3 sts,* (ss, ch4, dtr, ch4, ss) in next 5 sts, fasten off leaving a long tail. [12 petals]

Weave the starting tail in and out of the foundation ch and pull up tight to gather. Secure with a few stitches then take the yarn to the RS and sew the point of the first petal into the centre of the flower. Fasten off.

Small Flower
With Lemonade and a 3mm hook, ch8 leaving a long starting tail.
Repeat Row 1 of Large Flower [7 sts], then Row 2 up to *. Finish as for Large Flower.

Headband
With Chocolate and a 3mm hook, ch39.
Ss in second ch from hook and in each ch to end, fasten off and sew two ends together without twisting the band.

Sew the two flowers to one side of the Headband.

SASH
With Candy Apple and a 3mm hook, ch75.
Row 1 (RS) 2dc in second ch from hook, dc in each ch to last 2 ch, dc2tog, turn. [74 sts]
Row 2 Ch1, dc2tog, dc in each st to last 2 sts, 2dc in last st, fasten off. Fold Sash in half to find the centre, rejoin Candy Apple in the 12th st to the right of centre with a ss. Dc in back loops only of next 22 sts, ss in next st, ss across the surface of the back of the Sash to carry the yarn, ss in the st opposite on the other side, dc in back loops only (working in the other side of the foundation ch) of next 22 sts, ss in next st, fasten off and weave in ends.
The Sash will benefit from being blocked to stop it curling.

RED HANDBAG

Materials

■ Scheepjes Catona, Candy Apple (10g)

■ A 3mm hook

■ 30cm of Kreinik gold wired braid

■ Lining fabric (see note on page 11)

■ 2 red beads, 4mm

■ Sewing thread, or preferably metallic thread

■ Craft glue

See note about decreasing on page 10.

MAIN BAG

With Candy Apple and a 3mm hook, ch11.

Row 1 (RS) Dc in second ch from hook and in each ch to end, turn. [10 sts]

Row 2 Ch1, dc in each st to end, turn.

Row 3 Ch1, 2dc in first st, dc in each st to end, turn. [11 sts]

Row 4 As Row 3. [12 sts]

Rows 5-6 Ch1, dc in each st to end, turn.

Rows 7-10 Repeat last 4 rows. [14 sts]

Row 11 Ch1, dc in back loops only of each st to end, turn.

Rows 12-14 Ch1, dc in each st to end, turn.

Row 15 As Row 11.

Row 16 Ch1, dc in each st to end, turn.
Row 17 Ch1, dc in first st, dec, dc in each st to end, turn. [13 sts]
Row 18 As Row 17. [12 sts]
Rows 19-20 Ch1, dc in each st to end, turn.
Rows 21-24 Repeat last 4 rows. [10 sts]
Fasten off.

Gusset (Make 2)

In the following row it can be difficult to work into the ch following the one with 7 sts worked into it. You may wish to add an extra foundation chain or two at the start so that you can work in the next available ch after working this stitch. You can always undo any extra ch from the starting end if necessary.

With Candy Apple and a 3mm hook, ch23.
Row 1 (RS) Ss in second ch from hook and in next 11 ch, dc in next ch, htr in next 2 ch, (htr, tr, dtr, ch1, dtr, tr, htr) in next ch, htr in next 2 ch, dc in next ch, ss in next 3 ch, fasten off leaving a long tail for sewing.

Handles (Make 2)

With Candy Apple and a 3mm hook, ch19.
Row 1 Ss in second ch from hook and each ch to end, fasten off leaving a long tail.

TO MAKE UP

See Red Handbag Diagram on page 134.
If you want to line the handbag, draw around your Main Bag piece onto the lining fabric and cut inside the line to make the piece slightly smaller. Fold the fabric along the lines to match the rows of back loop dc that will form the folds in the bag.

Sew the first Gusset piece around the inside edge of the Main Bag, as shown in the Diagram. Before sewing the second piece, glue the lining in place to fit inside the lines of the Gusset; you may need to trim it to fit. Sew the second Gusset piece in position.

Wire and Beads

Put a small piece of tape over the end of the gold wired braid to make it easier to thread both beads onto the braid. Begin sewing the braid around the edge of the Gusset using sewing or metallic thread. Bend the beginning of the braid so that it looks like the shape shown on the first side of the Diagram; keep the starting piece before the loop as long as possible so that it's easier to bend as you can always trim it later. The loop and bead should be at least 1.5cm long so that you can twist both loops together to close the bag. Make sure the second bead sits at the top of the loop and sew the braid to the edge of the Gusset firmly at the base of the loop. Push the first bead ahead of you as you work and continue sewing the braid around the edge of the Gusset until you reach the centre-top on the second side. Make a second loop with bead as shown on the second side of the Diagram, and continue sewing the braid around until it reaches the first loop. Take the end of the braid past the first loop and tuck it underneath the Gusset to hide it. Trim both ends of the braid and put a blob of craft glue on the ends to stop them fraying. You'll need to make a sharp bend in the braid at the centre-bottom of the Gusset on each side and it's a good idea to add a blob of craft glue on each bend to stop the inside wire poking through the metallic outer braid.

Sew the Handles on each side of the bag using the image as a guide. The ending tail can be used to sew both ends of the Handle if you pass it under the Gusset on the inside.

DANCING SHOES
Materials
■ Scheepjes Catona, Candy Apple (5g)

■ A 2.5mm hook

■ 2 paper clips, 3cm long

■ Lining fabric for insoles (see note on page 11)

■ 2 mini white paper fasteners or small beads

■ 15cm of red cord elastic

■ Craft glue

■ Wire cutters

Note
These heeled shoes use a paper clip to enable you to bend the Sole into position. You can use a piece of lining fabric as an insole to cover the paper clip if you wish. If you choose to do this, draw around the Sole on the lining fabric to use as a guide before you complete the shoe.

SOLE AND UPPER
See Shoe Chart on page 134.

Sole
With Candy Apple and a 2.5mm hook, ch11 leaving a long starting tail. Work in a spiral without closing off each round with a ss.

Round 1 (RS) Htr in third ch from hook (counts as 2 htr), dc in next 5 ch, htr in next ch, tr in next ch, (tr, 4htr, tr) in next ch, rotate to work on other side of foundation ch, tr in next ch, htr in next ch, dc in next 5 ch, (2htr, 4tr) in next ch, do not fasten off. [28 sts]

Shoe Upper
Round 2 Ch1, working in back loops only; dc in top of beg ch-2, dc2tog, 4dc, dc2tog, 2dc, (2dc in next st) twice, 2dc, dc2tog, 4dc, dc2tog, 3dc, 2dc in next st, dc in last st. [27 sts]

Round 3 6dc, htr2tog, (tr3tog) twice, htr2tog, 11dc, ss in next st. [21 sts not including ss]

Round 4 Ss tightly in each st around until you reach the centre-front of the Shoe, then ch5, ss in second ch from hook and in each ch back to front of Shoe, ss in same st at base of ch and cont working ss around to end, fasten off. This forms the T-bar of the Dancing Shoe.

Once you've finished the Upper, the Shoe will probably be WS out because it has a tendency to pull this way when working. Leave it WS out and fasten off the tail of yarn, remembering to fasten off on the outside which will be the WS.

HEEL PIECE
With Candy Apple and a 2.5mm hook, ch4 leaving a long starting tail.

Row 1 Dc in second ch from hook and in next 2 ch, turn. [3 sts]

Row 2 Ch2 (does not count as st throughout), htr in st at base of ch, (dc, ss) in next st, turn leaving last st unworked.

Row 3 Ch1, skip ss, dc in dc, htr in htr, turn. [2 sts]

Row 4 Ch2, htr in st at base of ch, (dc, ss) in next st. Fasten off leaving a long tail.

TO MAKE UP

Taking a paper clip, straighten the outer piece of wire, getting rid of the first bend in the clip. Place this on the WS of the Sole with the straightened piece towards the Heel and the other end of the clip in line with the starting tail of yarn. Bend the straightened piece of the clip again, at the point where it meets the centre back of the heel, and push this end through the Sole. Using the starting tail, sew the paper clip to the Sole in this position. If you are adding insoles, put glue on the back of the insole and stick over the paper clip on the WS of the Sole and allow to dry before turning the Shoe RS out {1}.

Taking the Heel Piece, roll it up tightly so that the first row makes the length of the heel and the wider portion of the Heel Piece forms the wider top of the Heel. Use the ending tail of yarn to sew this in place and secure, but do not cut the end of the yarn yet {2}. Put the straightened end of the paper clip down the centre of the rolled up Heel Piece, and trim the end of the paper clip with wire cutters so that it finishes just before the end of the Heel Piece. The end of the paper clip will probably be showing at this point, so put some glue on the end of the heel and use the ending tail of yarn to bind the end of the heel piece, covering the paper clip. Add more glue to secure the binding and trim the end of yarn, gluing it in place. Bend the whole paper clip with the Sole so that it resembles the profile shown in the image {3}.

Use the starting tail of yarn on the Heel Piece to sew the top of the heel to the Sole, around the back of the heel {4}.

TO FINISH

See Dancing Shoe Diagram on page 134.
Add the paper fasteners/beads to the outside edge of each shoe as a mock fastening. Thread a piece of cord elastic on a large yarn needle and pass through the top of the T-bar on the underside, then back through the same place to make a small loop, being careful not to pull the loop back through. Put the loop of elastic over the paper fastener/bead, sewing in position if necessary. Take the two ends of the elastic and sew securely to the opposite inside of the Shoe, making sure that the piece of elastic is small enough so that you have to stretch it slightly to fit the foot.

are strengthened with fabric dressing tape on the reverse before stuffing and sewing together. You can use plastic toy filling granules at the base of the Radio to give it enough weight to stand. The Handle piece is worked around wired braid and attached to the Radio with paper fasteners.

FRONT AND BACK (MAKE 2)

With Cyan and a 3mm hook, ch16.
Row 1 (RS) Dc in second ch from hook and in each ch to end, turn. [15 sts]
Rows 2-9 Ch1, dc in each st to end, turn.
Row 10 Ch1, dc2tog, dc in each st to last 2 sts, dc2tog, turn. [13 sts]
Row 11 As Row 10. [11 sts]
Fasten off and weave in ends.

SIDES, TOP AND BASE

With Cyan and a 3mm hook, ch45 leaving a long starting tail.
Row 1 (RS) Dc in second ch from hook and in each ch to end, turn. [44 sts]
Rows 2-5 Ch1, dc in each st to end, turn.
Fasten off leaving a long tail.

Block all of the pieces with spray starch and leave them to dry.

FRONT DETAILS

With a strand of Jet Black, work lines of back stitch in between the rows on the Front piece. Leave the first st on the left unworked, and work each line for a length of 7 sts. There are 8 rows of stitching in total worked between Rows 2-10.

Dial

Layer the metallic button on top of the white button and stick in place using strong glue. Cut the legs from one of the brass paper fasteners with wire cutters, fold the remaining pieces inside the head of the fastener and stick this on top of the buttons in the centre with strong glue.

BERT'S RADIO
Materials

- Scheepjes Catona, Cyan (10g)
- Scheepjes Catona, Snow White (5g)
- A 60cm length of Scheepjes Catona, Jet Black
- A 3mm hook
- 22cm of Kreinik gold wired braid
- Metallic button, 14mm
- White button, 20mm
- 3 brass paper fasteners
- 2 mini white paper fasteners
- Curtain ring, 30mm
- Toy filling
- Plastic toy filling granules (optional)
- Sticky fabric dressing tape
- Craft glue
- Strong glue
- Spray starch
- Wire cutters

Note

The Radio is made from three main pieces; Front and Back (identical) and one piece which forms the Top/Base/Sides. The details are sewn or stuck in place and the pieces

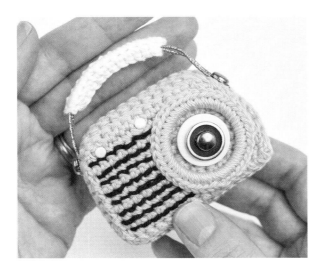

Take the curtain ring and work dc stitches into the ring with Cyan, working enough all around so that they cover the ring completely, ss to first dc, fasten off and weave in ends.

Stick the curtain ring to the right hand side on the Front with craft glue, lining it up with the right-hand edge and bottom. Stick the layered buttons in the centre of the ring with craft glue.
Put the two mini paper fasteners in position top left for the Radio buttons.

Put pieces of tape over the reverse of all the pieces to strengthen them before sewing them together. Split one of the tails of yarn on the Sides piece into two to use for sewing up. Position the end of the Sides piece at the centre bottom to hide the join, and sew this piece to the edges of the Front all around. It can help to mark the centre of the Sides piece so that you can make sure you're aligning it accurately as you sew, because you can make sure that this point matches the centre-top.

Sew the join of the Sides piece together at the base. If needed, you can use the other half of the split tail of yarn to sew the join, but otherwise fasten this off and weave in the ends. Before sewing the Back piece make the Handle for the Radio as follows:

Handle
Put the other two brass paper fasteners on each side at the top. Bend the length of wired braid around each fastener and fold double so that the ends meet in the centre. Remove it from the fasteners with the bends in place and work around the Radio handle as follows:

With Snow White and a 3mm hook, ch 13.
Row 1 Dc in second ch from hook and in each ch to end, turn. [12 sts]
Row 2 Ch 1, dc in each st to end, turn.
Row 3 Ch 1, insert the hook into the back loop only of the next st and into the first rem loop of the foundation ch at the same time, before completing a dc stitch. Work this around the piece of braid so that the rows form a tube encasing the braid with the last row joined to the first. Work a dc st in the same way in the rest of the sts, fasten off and weave in ends. Replace the Handle on the fasteners.

TO FINISH
Complete the seam between the Back and Sides pieces, carefully adding a little toy filling and plastic toy filling granules to add weight (optional) before you complete the seam, fasten off and weave in ends.

chapter eight:
betty goes shopping

Betty can't leave the house without looking the part, especially if she's going shopping. Co-ordinated accessories are the must-have of the season. Shopping isn't really Bert's thing, but if a cat must lounge about he can do it in style, with his French beret and scarf keeping him warm in the coldest weather

Total yarn quantities for this section: Scheepjes Catona 35g of Saffron (249), 45g of Linen (505), 30g of Chocolate (507), 20g of Jet Black (110), 10g of Cyan (397). Check the yarn quantities needed for all projects on page 121.

betty's shopping ensemble

Leopard print is all the rage don't you know, so there are touches on her hat, handbag and cape collar to bring her outfit together. Her cape is fastened at the front with a jewellery clasp, but you could use a button or ribbon if that's easier

Materials
- Scheepjes Catona, Saffron (35g)
- Scheepjes Catona, Linen (10g)
- A 3mm hook
- T-bar and loop fastening (from a jewellery supplier)
- Chain link or jump ring (optional)
- Sewing thread

For Leopard Print Effect
- Wire brush
- Fine black permanent marker
- Yellow ochre coloured pencil, preferably watercolour

Note
The Cape is made from side to side in rows, with a gap at the front on each side for the arms. The Collar is added afterwards. Keep the slip stitches a little loose throughout otherwise they become difficult to work into on the following row. The last slip stitch of the row can be tricky; try using a smaller hook for this stitch to make it easier to insert the hook.

BETTY'S CAPE

Front

Back

111

Right Front

With Saffron and a 3mm hook, ch33.

Row 1 (RS) Ss in second ch from hook and next 7 ch, 8dc, 8htr, 8tr, turn. [32 sts]

Row 2 Ch1, working in back loops only; 24dc, 8ss, turn.

Row 3 Ch1, working in back loops only; 8ss, 8dc, 8htr, 8tr, turn.

Rows 4-14 Repeat Rows 2 and 3 five more times, then repeat Row 2 once more.

Back

Row 15 Ch1, working in back loops only; 8ss, 4dc, ch20, turn.

Row 16 Ch1, dc in second ch from hook and next 19 ch, working in back loops only; 4dc, 8ss, turn.

Row 17 As Row 3.

Rows 18-54 Repeat Rows 2 and 3 a further 18 times, then repeat Row 2 once more.

Left Front

Rows 55-57 Repeat Rows 15-17.

Rows 58-69 Repeat Rows 2 and 3 six more times, fasten off and weave in ends.

COLLAR

With Linen and a 3mm hook, ch7.

Row 1 (WS) Dc in second ch from hook and in each ch to end, turn. [6 sts]

Row 2 Ch1, ss in first 2 sts, dc in each st to end, turn.

Row 3 Ch1, dc in each st to end, working in the front loops only of the ss if it helps to work these more easily.

Rows 4-45 Repeat Rows 2 and 3 a further 21 times, or until Collar fits around top of Cape.

Fasten off leaving a long tail. Weave in the starting tail, then thread the finishing tail onto a needle and work a running stitch along the WS neckline edge of the Collar to gather it slightly to fit the neckline edge.

Leopard Print Effect

Use the wire brush to brush the RS of the Collar until the stitches are less distinct and it becomes 'furry'. With the black pen, draw markings on the collar, as shown in the Leopard Print Illustration on page 135. Fill in some of these markings with the yellow ochre pencil. You'll get a better colour if you use a water colour pencil and dampen the end slightly.

Using sewing thread, sew the Collar to the Cape at the neckline. To get a more authentic effect fold the top edge of the Collar slightly, and sew to the inside edge of the neckline.

Sew the loop of the fastening to one side of the top of the Cape. The T-bar will be sewn to the opposite side, but there needs to be a bit of space between the T-bar and the fabric. I attached a chain link to the T-bar before sewing it to the other side of the Cape, but you could use a loop of thread.

SKIRT

Materials

▪ Scheepjes Catona, Chocolate (25g)

▪ A 3mm hook

▪ 1 button, 5mm

Note

The Skirt is worked from side to side, starting at the centre back. The first and last rows are joined in part, to leave an opening at the top, and a split at the bottom. In the (dc, ch1) rib pattern beg in Row 2, ch always count as sts and total st count remains constant until you reach the Underlap.

With Chocolate and a 3mm hook, ch32.

Row 1 (WS) Dc in second ch from hook and in each ch to end, turn. [31 sts]

Row 2 Ch1, (dc in next st, ch1, skip next st) repeat to last st, dc in last st, turn. [31 sts including ch]

Row 3 As Row 2, do not fasten off.

Shaping Rows

The shaping rows have 8 slip stitches worked in back loops only at the waist edge of the Skirt; the rest is

Front

worked in the rib pattern as set by Row 2. On a RS row the slip stitches will be the first 8 sts of the row, on a WS row they'll be the last 8 sts of the row:

Row 4 (RS) Ch1, (dc in next dc, ch1, skip next ch) repeat to last 8 sts, ss in back loops of last 8 sts, turn.

Row 5 (WS) Ch1, ss in back loops only of first 8 sts, then working in both loops as usual; (dc in next dc, ch1, skip next ch) repeat to last st, dc in last dc, turn.

Rows 6-7 As Rows 4-5.

Row 8 As Row 4.

Rows 9-14 As Row 2.

Rows 15-19 Work shaping rows as described above, with 8 ss at the waist edge of the Skirt.

Rows 20-42 Work (6 rib rows as Row 2, 5 Shaping Rows) twice.

Rows 43-45 As Row 2.

Do not fasten off.

Underlap for Skirt

This is an extra piece continued for part of the row, that will extend underneath the split opening at the bottom of the Skirt.

Row 46 (RS) Work in rib patt as Row 2 for first 12 sts, ss in next st, turn leaving rem sts unworked. [13 sts including ss]

Row 47 Skip ss, ss in next ch-1 sp, (dc in next st, ch1, skip next st) repeat to last st, dc in last st, turn. [12 sts including ss]

Row 48 Work in rib patt as Row 2 for first 11 sts, ss in row ends of previous 2 rows, fasten off leaving a long tail for sewing.

Back

Use the long tail to sew together the first and last rows over the next 8 sts, fasten off leaving an opening at the top of the Skirt. Sew the top of the Skirt Underlap to the WS.

WAISTBAND

Rejoin Chocolate with a dc to centre back waist edge at top of Skirt with WS facing. Dc evenly across top of Skirt, turn, ch1, and dc in each st across, ch4 for a button loop and ss to end of first row of Waistband, fasten off and weave in ends.

Sew button to other end of Waistband opposite button loop.

Block to stop the curl at the hem edges of the Skirt.

BLOUSE

Materials
■ Scheepjes Catona, Linen (20g)

■ 4 pearl beads or buttons, 5mm

■ A 3mm hook

See note about decreasing on page 10.

Note
The Sleeves are made first and set aside. The Body of the Blouse is worked bottom up and then the Sleeves are joined in and the Yoke worked as one piece.

SLEEVES (MAKE 2)
With Linen and a 3mm hook, ch11 leaving a long starting tail.

Row 1 (RS) Dc in second ch from hook and in each ch to end, turn. [10 sts]

Rows 2-3 Ch1, dc in each st to end, turn.

Row 4 Ch1, 2dc in first st, dc in each st to end, turn. [11 sts]

Rows 5-7 Ch1, dc in each st to end, turn.

Row 8 Ch1, dc in each st to last st, 2dc in last st, turn. [12 sts]

Rows 9-11 As Row 2.

Row 12 As Row 4. [13 sts]

Rows 13-16 Repeat Rows 5-8. [14 sts after Row 16] Fasten off leaving a long tail. Use the starting tail to sew the Sleeve seam.

BODY
With Linen and a 3mm hook, ch26.

Row 1 (RS) Ch1, dc in each st to end, turn. [25 sts]

Row 2 Ch1, 4dc, 2dc in next st, 3dc, 2dc in next st, 7dc, 2dc in next st, 3dc, 2dc in next st, 4dc, turn. [29 sts]

Row 3 Ch1, (4dc, 2dc in next st) twice, 9dc, (2dc in next st, 4dc) twice, turn. [33 sts]

Row 4 Ch1, (5dc, 2dc in next st) twice, 9dc, (2dc in next st, 5dc) twice, turn. [37 sts]

Row 5 Ch1, 6dc, 2dc in next st, 5dc, 2dc in next st, 11dc, 2dc in next st, 5dc, 2dc in next st, 6dc, turn. [41 sts]

Row 6 Ch1, 10dc, 2dc in next st, 19dc, 2dc in next st, 10dc, turn. [43 sts]

Rows 7-10 Ch1, dc in each st to end, turn, do not fasten off.

Joining in Sleeves

Row 11 Ch1, 8dc, *holding Sleeve with seam underneath, dc in 9 uppermost sts of Sleeve, skip next 5 sts on Body**, dc in next 17 sts on Body, repeat from * to ** with other Sleeve, dc in last 8 sts on Body, turn. [51 working sts]

Row 12 Ch1, (7dc, dec) twice, 15dc, (dec, 7dc) twice, turn. [47 sts]

Row 13 Ch1, (6dc, dec) twice, 15dc, (dec, 6dc) twice, turn. [43 sts]

Row 14 Ch1, 6dc, dec, 4dc, dec, 15dc, dec, 4dc, dec, 6dc, turn. [39 sts]

Row 15 Ch1, 6dc, dec, 3dc, dec, 13dc, dec, 3dc, dec, 6dc, turn. [35 sts]

Row 16 Ch1, 5dc, dec, 3dc, dec, 11dc, dec, 3dc, dec, 5dc, turn. [31 sts]

Row 17 Ch1, 4dc, dec, 3dc, dec, 9dc, dec, 3dc, dec, 4dc, turn. [27 sts]

Row 18 Ch1, 4dc, dec, 13dc, dec, 6dc, turn, do not fasten off. [25 sts]

Collar

Row 19 Ch1, 8dc in front loops only, dec, 5dc, dec, 8dc in front loops only, turn. [23 sts]

Row 20 Ch1, 8dc in back loops only, skip next st,

5dc, skip next st, 8dc in back loops only, turn. [21 sts]
Row 21 Ch1, working in front loops only for the whole row; 6dc, (2dc in next st, 1dc) twice, 1dc, (1dc, 2dc in next st) twice, 6dc. [25 sts]
Row 22 Ch1, dc in each st to end, fasten off leaving a long tail.
Use the long tail to sew down the point of the Collar, and to sew the edge of the Collar in position along the back neck to the other point of the Collar, fasten off on WS.
From WS, use the ending tails of the Sleeves to sew up the gap at each underarm.
Weave in all ends.

Buttonholes
Rejoin Linen to the bottom right front with RS facing.
Row 1 (RS) Ch1, dc in first row end, ch1, skip next row end, (dc in next 2 row ends, ch1, skip next row end) 3 times, dc in next row end, ss in next row end, fasten off and weave in ends. [4 buttonholes made]
Sew buttons or beads to left front to match the buttonholes.

The Blouse will benefit from being sprayed with water and blocked to help it lie flat.

HIGH-HEELED SHOES
Materials
▨ Scheepjes Catona, Jet Black (5g)

▨ A 2.5mm hook

▨ 2 paper clips, 3cm long

▨ Craft glue

▨ Lining fabric for insoles (see note on page 11)

▨ Wire cutters

Note
These Shoes follow the same pattern as the Dancing Shoes on page 104 except that they're worked in Jet Black throughout, and don't have the T-bar of the Dancing Shoes. Follow the instructions for the Dancing Shoes, replacing

Round 4 of the Upper with the following:

Round 4 Ss tightly in each st around, fasten off and weave in ends.

Continue to follow the Dancing Shoes instructions for the Heel Piece and Making Up, but leave out the finishing details which relate to the T-bar.

LEOPARD PRINT HANDBAG
Materials
▨ Scheepjes Catona, Jet Black (10g)

▨ Scheepjes Catona, Linen (5g)

▨ A 3mm hook

▨ Kreinik gold wired braid, 30cm

▨ Sewing thread, or preferably gold metallic thread

▨ Lining fabric (see note on page 11)

▨ Craft glue

For Leopard Print Effect
▨ Wire brush

▨ Fine black permanent marker

▨ Yellow ochre coloured pencil, preferably watercolour

See note about decreasing on page 10.

MAIN BAG
With Jet Black and a 3mm hook, ch11.
Row 1 (RS) Dc in second ch from hook and in each ch to end, turn. [10 sts]
Row 2 Ch1, dc in each st to end, turn.
Row 3 Ch1, 2dc in first st, dc in each st to end, turn. [11 sts]
Row 4 As Row 3. [12 sts]
Rows 5-10 Ch1, dc in each st to end, turn.
Row 11 Ch1, dc in back loops only of each st to end, turn.
Rows 12-14 Ch1, dc in each st to end, turn.
Row 15 As Row 11.
Rows 16-20 Ch1, dc in each st to end, turn.
Row 21 Ch1, dec, dc in each rem st to end, turn. [11 sts]

Row 22 As Row 21. [10 sts]
Rows 23-24 Ch1, dc in each st to end, fasten off.

Gusset (Make 2)

In the following row it can be difficult to work into the ch following the one with 7 sts worked into it. You may wish to add an extra foundation chain or two at the start so that you can work in the next available ch after working this stitch. You can always undo any extra ch from the starting end if necessary.
With Jet Black and a 3mm hook, ch23.
Row 1 (RS) Ss in second ch from hook and in next 11 ch, dc in next ch, htr in next 2 ch, (htr, tr, dtr, ch1, dtr, tr, htr) in next ch, htr in next 2 ch, dc in next ch, ss in next 3 ch, fasten off leaving a long tail.

Handles (Make 2)

With Jet Black and a 3mm hook, ch19.
Row 1 Ss in second ch from hook and in each ch to end, fasten off leaving a long tail.

Leopard Print Panel (Make 2)

With Linen and a 3mm hook, ch9.
Row 1 (RS) Dc in second ch from hook and in each ch to end, turn. [8 sts]
Row 2 Ch1, 4dc, 2dc in next st, 3dc, turn. [9 sts]
Rows 3-8 Ch1, dc in each st to end, turn.
Fasten off leaving a long tail.
Repeat the process for creating the Leopard Print Effect on the RS of each Panel as described for the Collar of the Cape on page 112.

TO MAKE UP

Sew the Leopard Print Panels on each side of the Handbag with the last row aligned with the base. If you split the ending tail you can use this thread to sew finer stitches; use one half of the thread to work around two sides of the panel in one direction, and the other half to sew around the remaining two sides in the other direction.

If you want to line the Handbag, draw around your Main Bag piece and cut inside the line to make the piece slightly smaller. Fold the fabric along the lines to match the rows of back loop dc that will form the folds in the Main Bag piece.

Sew the first Gusset piece around the inside edge of the Main Bag using sewing or metallic thread as shown in the Leopard Print Handbag Diagram on page 135. Before sewing the second piece, glue the lining in place to fit inside the lines of the Gusset; you may need to trim it to fit. Sew the second Gusset piece in position.

Taking the gold wired braid, sew over the braid using sewing or metallic thread and working around the edge of the Gusset piece. Start the braid at the top of the Gusset on the first side, leaving as much braid as possible before you make a loop for the centre fastening. You can trim the start of the braid later if it's too long. Make a loop at the centre top on the second side for the fastening, as shown in the Leopard Print Handbag Diagram on page 135.

On the second side, make the loop first and secure firmly with stitches at the base before winding the braid around the base of the first loop to create a second loop. This will enable you to fasten the bag, as the loop on the other side can be pushed up through this second loop to hold it in place. Sew the second loop firmly before finishing the round with the braid, taking the end of the braid past the first loop and hiding the end of the braid underneath the Gusset. Trim both ends of the braid and put a blob of craft glue on the ends to stop them fraying. You'll need to make a sharp bend in the braid at the centre bottom of the Gusset on each side and it's a good idea to add a blob of glue on each bend to stop the inside wire poking through the metallic outer braid.

Sew the Handles on each side of the bag using the image as a guide. The ending tail can be used to sew both ends of the Handle if you pass it under the Gusset on the inside.

HAT AND HAIR
Materials
- Scheepjes Catona, Linen (10g)
- Scheepjes Catona, Jet Black (5g)
- Scheepjes Catona, Chocolate (5g)
- A 3mm hook
- Plastic milk bottle lid or similar measuring 4cm diameter
- Masking tape
- Toy filling
- Old tights
- Black shirring elastic and hook and loop fastening if you want the Hat/Hair to be removable
- Craft glue

For Leopard Print Effect
- Wire brush
- Fine black permanent marker
- Yellow ochre coloured pencil, preferably watercolour

See note about decreasing on page 10.

Note
The Hat and Hair are made as one piece with the Hair sewn inside the back of the Hat.

HAT
Work in a spiral without closing off each round with a ss.
With Linen and a 3mm hook, make a magic loop.
Round 1 (RS) Ch1, 6dc into loop. [6 sts]
Round 2 2dc in each st around. [12 sts]
Round 3 (1dc, 2dc in next st) 6 times. [18 sts]
Round 4 (2dc, 2dc in next st) 6 times. [24 sts]
Round 5 (3dc, 2dc in next st) 6 times. [30 sts]
Round 6 (4dc, 2dc in next st) 6 times. [36 sts]
Round 7 Ss in next st and ch1 to make this stitch the new start of the round, closing off each round with a ss from now on. Dc in each st around, ss to first dc.
Round 8 Ch1, dc in each st around, ss to first dc.
Round 9 Ch1, dec, dc in each rem st around, ss to first dc. [35 sts]
Round 10 Ch1, dc in each st around, ss to first dc.
Round 11 Working in back loops only; ch1, 10dc, 2htr, 2htr in next st, 2htr, (1tr, 2tr in next st) twice, tr in next st, 2htr, 2htr in next st, 2htr, 10dc, ss to first dc. [39 sts]
Round 12 Ch1, (9dc, 2dc in next st) 3 times, 8dc, 2dc in last st, ss to first dc. [43 sts]
Round 13 Ch1, 5dc, 2dc in next st, (10dc, 2dc in next st) 3 times, 4dc, ss to first dc, fasten off. [47 sts]

Repeat the instructions on page 112 for making the Leopard Print Effect on the crown and the brim of the Hat, which is better to complete before adding the following edging round. You can leave the portion which will be underneath the Hat Band.
Join Jet Black in the first st of the round.
Round 14 Ch1, dc in each st around, fasten off and weave in ends.

HAT BAND
With Jet Black and a 3mm hook, ch35.
Row 1 (RS) Dc in second ch from hook and in each ch to end, turn. [34 sts]
Rows 2-3 Ch1, dc in each st to end, turn.

Fasten off leaving a long tail, and use the tail to sew together the two short ends of the Hat Band.

TO MAKE UP
With Linen, run a gathering thread around Round 10 of the crown leaving the ends unsecured for the moment. The crown of the Hat is filled with toy filling, and then the plastic lid will be stuck inside with the top uppermost, so that the bottom edges of the lid are aligned with Round 10 at the bottom of the crown. It helps to put the toy filling inside a piece of tights or similar, so that it is contained and doesn't escape down the sides of the plastic lid. Wrap masking tape around the edge of the lid so that it sticks more easily with glue. Put the filling in place at the top and glue around the inside bottom edges of the crown where the lid will sit. Put the lid in position and draw up the gathering thread to fit the lid tightly and sticking the inside of the Hat to the edges of the lid. Secure the ends of the gathering thread and fasten off.
Put the Hat Band over the crown.

HAIR
The Hair is made in three pieces and sewn to the inside brim of the Hat. Refer to the Hat and Hair Diagram on page 135.

Back Piece
With Chocolate and a 3mm hook, ch8 leaving a long starting tail.
Row 1 2htr in second ch from hook (skipped first ch does not count as st), htr in next ch, 3dc, 2ss, turn. [8 sts]
Working in back loops only throughout:
Row 2 Ch1, 2ss, 4dc, 2htr, turn.
Row 3 Ch1, 2htr in first st, htr in next st, 4dc, 2ss, turn. [9 sts]
Row 4 Ch1, 2ss, 5dc, 2htr, turn.
Row 5 Ch1, 2htr in first st, htr in next st, 5dc, 2ss, turn. [10 sts]

Row 6 Ch1, 2ss, 6dc, 2htr, turn.
Row 7 Ch1, 2htr in first st, htr in next st, 6dc, 2ss, turn. [11 sts]
Row 8 Ch1, 2ss, 7dc, 2htr, turn.
Row 8 forms the centre back. From now on, the rows are a mirror image of the previous rows.
Row 9 Ch1, htr2tog, htr in next st, 6dc, 2ss, turn. [10 sts]
Row 10 As Row 6.
Row 11 Ch1, htr2tog, htr in next st, 5dc, 2ss, turn. [9 sts]
Row 12 As Row 4.
Row 13 Ch1, htr2tog, htr in next st, 4dc, 2ss, turn. [8 sts]
Row 14 As Row 2.
Row 15 Ch1, htr2tog, htr in next st, 3dc, 2ss, fasten off, leaving a long tail.
Use the ending tail to run a thread through the ss ends of the rows, pulling it up tight and securing the thread so the Hair Piece makes a semi-circular shape with the first, and the last rows forming the flat edge of the semi-circle. Don't fasten off this thread yet.

Side Pieces (make 2)
With Chocolate and a 3mm hook, ch5 leaving a long starting tail.
Row 1 Ss in second ch from hook, ss in next ch, dc in next ch, htr in next ch, ch4, ss in second ch from hook

and in next 2 ch, fasten off and weave in end. Use the starting tail to sew this piece to the corner of the Back Hair Piece (see Hat and Hair Diagram on page 135). Turn the second Side Piece over and sew to the opposite corner. If you're sewing the Hat/Hair to the Head, pin in position on Betty and sew the Hair first, followed by the Hat.

If making the Hat/Hair removable, put them on Betty, adjust the position so that the Side Pieces fit around the Ears and pin in position. Tack in place from the RS, using a piece of contrasting waste thread, being careful not to sew through the Head. Remove and sew the Hair to the inside of the Hat from the WS, starting at the centre and using each tail to work from the centre out. When you reach the side pieces, double check the position before sewing in place. Remove the tacking yarn. Stick a piece of hook and loop fastening to the inside of the Hat on the plastic lid and run a double length of shirring elastic around the inside edge of the Back Hair Piece.

BERT'S BERET AND SCARF

Materials
▨ Scheepjes Catona, Cyan (10g)
▨ A 3mm hook

HAT
Work in a spiral without closing off each round with a ss. With Cyan and a 3mm hook, make a magic loop leaving a long starting tail.

Round 1 (RS) Ch1, 6dc into loop. [6 sts]
Round 2 2dc in each st around. [12 sts]
Round 3 (1dc, 2dc in next st) 6 times. [18 sts]
Round 4 (2dc, 2dc in next st) 6 times. [24 sts]
Round 5 (3dc, 2dc in next st) 6 times. [30 sts]
Round 6 (4dc, 2dc in next st) 6 times. [36 sts]
Round 7 Dc in each st around.
Round 8 (4dc, dec) 6 times. [30 sts]
Round 9 (3dc, dec) 6 times. [24 sts]

Round 10 Ss in each st around, fasten off and weave in ending tail.
Thread the starting tail through the centre to the RS and make a slip knot on the hook as close as possible to the Hat. Ch5, fasten off and pass the end back through the centre to secure. Weave in ends.

SCARF
With Cyan and a 3mm hook, ch41 leaving a starting tail of approx 40cm.
Row 1 Dc in second ch from hook and in each ch to end, turn. [40 sts]
Row 2 Ch1, dc in each st to end, fasten off leaving a tail of approx 40cm.

Thread the starting tail on a needle and insert back into the end of the Scarf to create a small loop (approx 1cm long). Pass the end back through the loop and secure with a small stitch at the base. Repeat to create several loops along the end of the Scarf then cut the loops to create a fringe. Repeat at the other end of the Scarf with the finishing tail.

abbreviations

(UK terms used throughout)

Beg Beginning

Ch Chain

Ch-sp Chain space

Ch-3 sp Chain space containing 3 chain (or the number shown)

Dc Double crochet

Dc2tog Work 2 double crochet stitches together (decrease 1 stitch): (insert hook in next st/sp, pull up loop) twice, yrh, draw through both loops on hook

Dec Decrease (see note on page 10)

Htr Half treble crochet

Htr2tog Work 2 half treble stitches together (decrease 1 stitch): (yrh, insert hook in next st/sp, yrh, pull up loop) twice, yrh, draw through all loops on hook

Htr3tog Work 3 half treble stitches together (decrease 2 stitches): As for htr2tog, working () 3 times.

Rem Remaining

Rep Repeat

*....; rep from * x more times Repeat everything between ; and * so many more times

(...) x times Work the instruction between the brackets the total number of times stated. Also used when more than one stitch type is worked in the same stitch or sp, eg '(dc, ch1) in next st'.

RS Right side

Sp(s) Space (s)

Ss Slip stitch

St(s) Stitch(es)

Tr Treble crochet

Tr2tog Work 2 treble stitches together (decrease 1 stitch): (yrh, insert hook in next st/sp, pull up loop, yrh, draw through 2 loops) twice, yrh draw through all loops on hook

Tr3tog Work 3 treble stitches together (decrease 2 stitches): As for tr2tog, working () 3 times.

[..] Square brackets at the end of row/round show the stitch count.

WS Wrong side

Yrh Yarn round hook

yarn list & stockists

YARN LIST FOR ALL PROJECTS

Scheepjes Catona, 100% cotton
Catona is available in 50g, 25g and 10g balls. The yarn quantities are listed to the nearest 25g, except in the case where 10 or fewer grams are needed, then a 10g ball is stated.

Apple Green (513) 50g
Candy Apple (516) 150g
Chocolate (507) 100g
Chrystalline (385) 100g
Cyan (397) 75g
Delphinium (113) 50g
Lemonade (403) 50g
Lilac Mist (399) 100g
Linen (505) 50g
Jet Black (110) 150g
Nude (255) 75g
Rose Wine (396) 10g
Saffron (249) 50g
Soft Rose (409) 50g
Snow White (106) 125g

Scheepjes Maxi Sweet Treat
(100% cotton, 25g/140m)
Lemonade (403) 25g
Soft Rose (409) 25g

Scheepjes Panda
(100% polyester, 50g/90m)
Husky (583) 50g

Gold lurex yarn 5g

STOCKISTS AND USEFUL CONTACTS

caramedus.com

scheepjes.com

Most of the materials are available in general craft supply stores, but there are a few more specific items listed here:

Kreinik gold wired braid
lakesideneedlecraft.co.uk

Darice 7HPI ultra stiff plastic canvas
minervacrafts.com

Plastic (polypropylene) toy granules
fredaldous.co.uk

Mice Print Cotton Poplin Fabric, Aqua Blue (Rose and Hubble)
minervacrafts.com

HEEL CIRCLE DIAGRAM

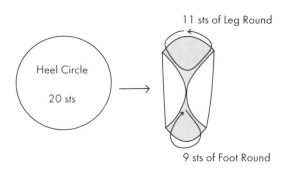

11 sts of Leg Round

Heel Circle

20 sts

9 sts of Foot Round

HIP TO WAIST CHART

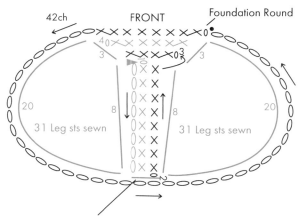

42ch

FRONT

Foundation Round

40

3

3

20

20

31 Leg sts sewn

31 Leg sts sewn

8

8

KEY

• Slip stitch (ss)
◯ Chain (ch)
✕ Double crochet (dc)
✕✕ 2dc in same stitch
▶ Start
→ Direction of work

These 2 sts to be sewn to end of gusset rows once Leg and central wires are joined

JOINING LEGS DIAGRAM

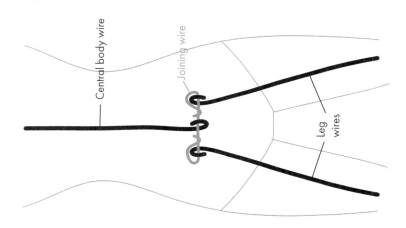

Central body wire

Joining wire

Leg wires

FACE DIAGRAM

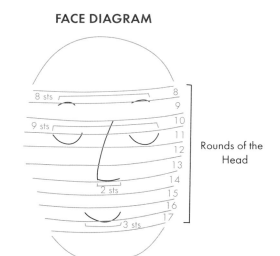

8 sts

8

9

9 sts

10

11

12

13

14

2 sts

15

16

3 sts

17

Rounds of the Head

BUST CHART

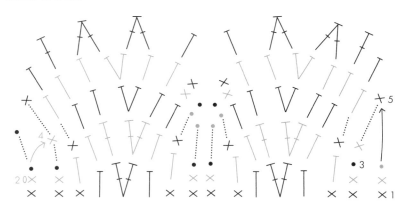

5

4

3

20

1

KEY

• Slip stitch (ss)
◯ Chain (ch)
✕ Double crochet (dc)

T Half treble crochet (htr)

┬ Treble crochet (tr)

⋀ Tr2tog

┊ Shows where stitch is to be worked

→ Direction of work

ARM DIAGRAM

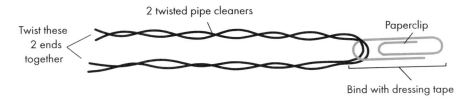

Twist these 2 ends together

2 twisted pipe cleaners

Paperclip

Bind with dressing tape

HAIR IN A BUN CHART

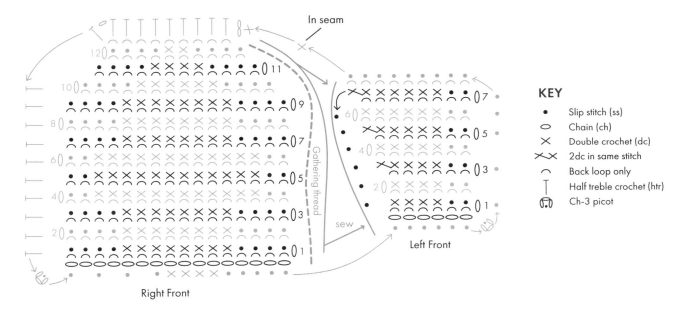

In seam

Gathering thread

sew

Left Front

Right Front

KEY

- • Slip stitch (ss)
- ○ Chain (ch)
- ✕ Double crochet (dc)
- ⋊ 2dc in same stitch
- ⌒ Back loop only
- T Half treble crochet (htr)
- ⊙ Ch-3 picot

BRA CHART

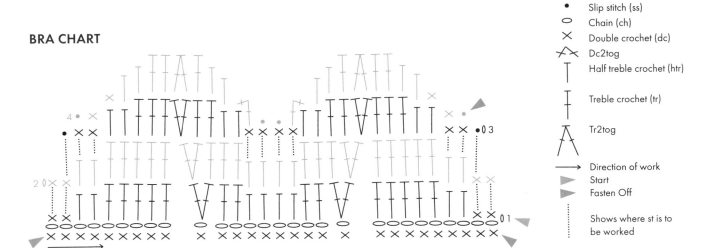

KEY

- • Slip stitch (ss)
- ○ Chain (ch)
- ✕ Double crochet (dc)
- ⋏ Dc2tog
- T Half treble crochet (htr)
- ⊤ Treble crochet (tr)
- ⋀ Tr2tog
- → Direction of work
- ▶ Start
- ▶ Fasten Off
- ⋮ Shows where st is to be worked

LOW-HEELED SHOE CHART

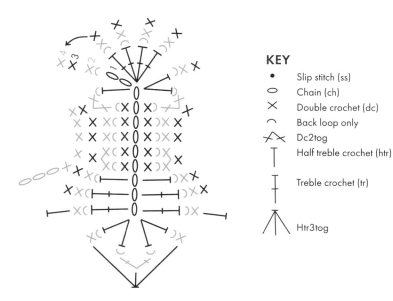

KEY

•	Slip stitch (ss)
○	Chain (ch)
✕	Double crochet (dc)
⌒	Back loop only
⋏	Dc2tog
T	Half treble crochet (htr)
‡	Treble crochet (tr)
⋔	Htr3tog

FRONT LEG PIECE DIAGRAM

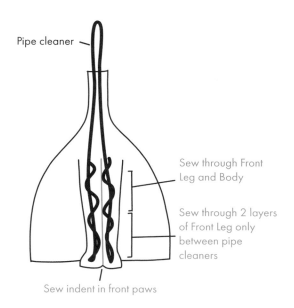

Pipe cleaner

Sew through Front Leg and Body

Sew through 2 layers of Front Leg only between pipe cleaners

Sew indent in front paws

TAIL AND BACK PAWS CHART

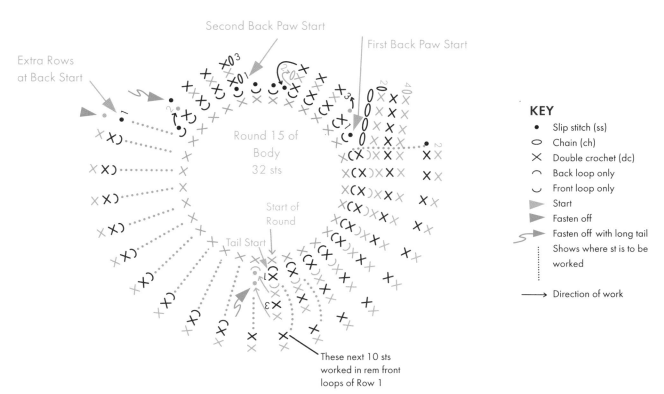

Extra Rows at Back Start

Second Back Paw Start

First Back Paw Start

Round 15 of Body 32 sts

Start of Round

Tail Start

These next 10 sts worked in rem front loops of Row 1

KEY

•	Slip stitch (ss)
○	Chain (ch)
✕	Double crochet (dc)
⌒	Back loop only
⌣	Front loop only
▶	Start
▶	Fasten off
↪	Fasten off with long tail
⋮	Shows where st is to be worked
→	Direction of work

SHEATH DRESS
SHOULDER BAND DIAGRAM

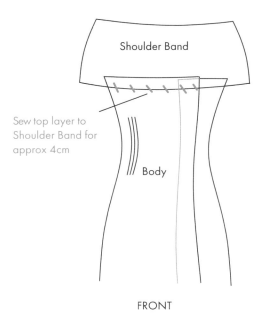

Sew top layer to Shoulder Band for approx 4cm

Shoulder Band

Body

FRONT

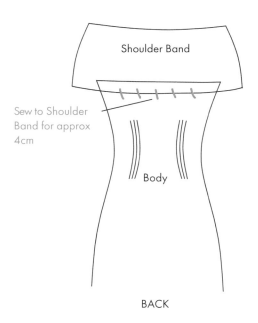

Sew to Shoulder Band for approx 4cm

Shoulder Band

Body

BACK

EVENING GOWN TRAIN DIAGRAM

1.

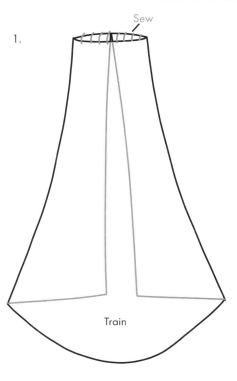

Sew

Train

2.

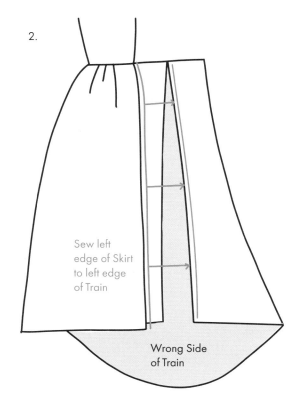

Sew left edge of Skirt to left edge of Train

Wrong Side of Train

3.

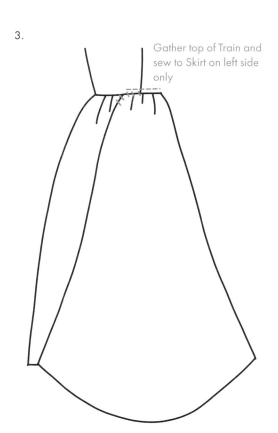

Gather top of Train and sew to Skirt on left side only

4.

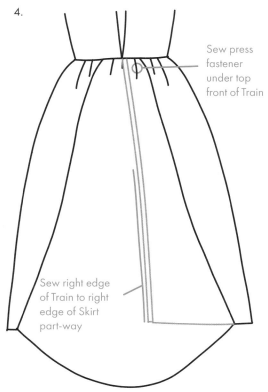

Sew press fastener under top front of Train

Sew right edge of Train to right edge of Skirt part-way

CAPRI PANTS CHART

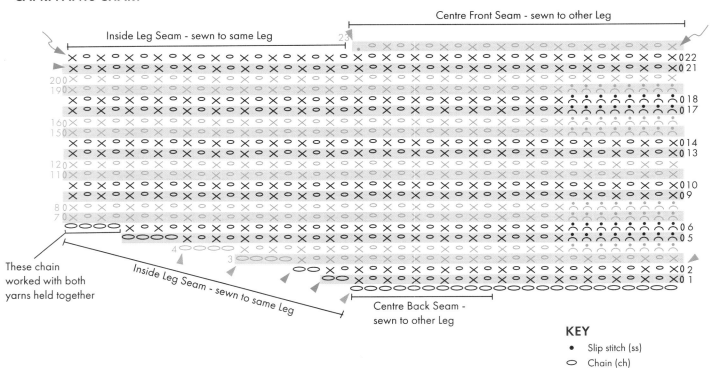

Centre Front Seam - sewn to other Leg

Inside Leg Seam - sewn to same Leg

These chain worked with both yarns held together

Inside Leg Seam - sewn to same Leg

Centre Back Seam - sewn to other Leg

WAISTLINE EDGE

BERT'S LEGS DIAGRAM

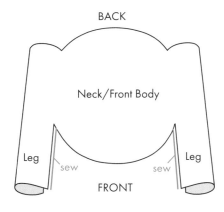

BACK

Neck/Front Body

Leg

sew

Leg

sew

FRONT

BERT'S BACK BODY DIAGRAM

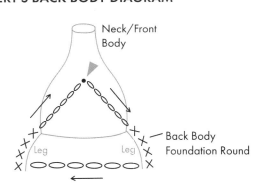

Neck/Front Body

Back Body Foundation Round

Leg

Leg

FRONT FLAP DIAGRAM

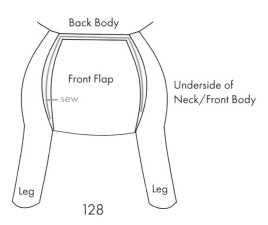

Back Body

Front Flap

sew

Underside of Neck/Front Body

Leg

Leg

KEY

- • Slip stitch (ss)
- ⌀ Chain (ch)
- ✕ Double crochet (dc)
- ⌒ Back loop only
- ▶ Start
- ▶ Fasten o ff
- ↝ Fasten o ff with long tail

□ Snow White

▨ Jet Black

SWIMSUIT CUPS CHART

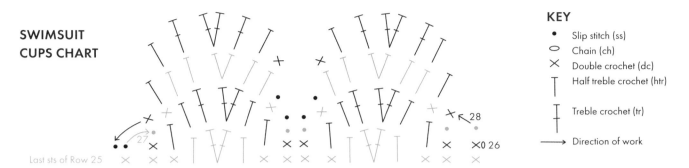

KEY

- • Slip stitch (ss)
- ⬭ Chain (ch)
- ✕ Double crochet (dc)
- | Half treble crochet (htr)
- ‡ Treble crochet (tr)
- → Direction of work

HEADSCARF DIAGRAM

SWIMSUIT DIAGRAM

HAIR PIECE DIAGRAM

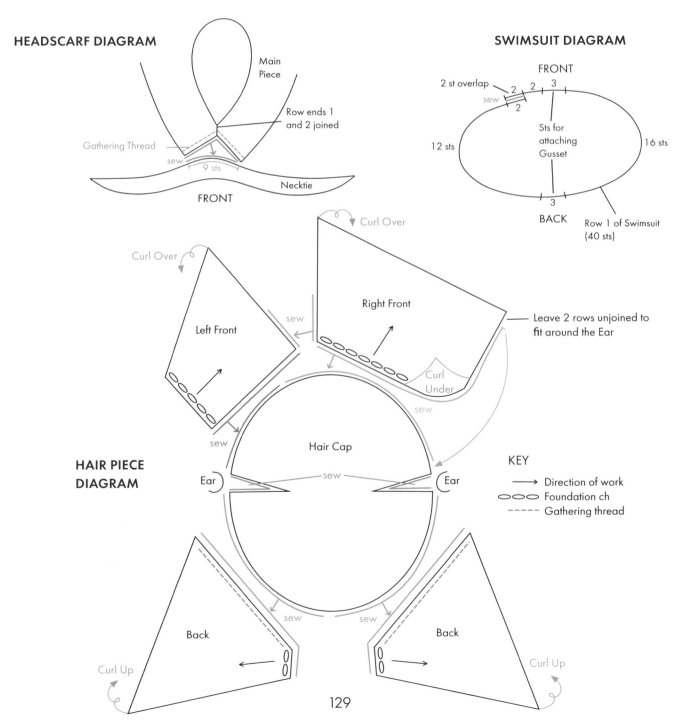

KEY

- → Direction of work
- ⬭⬭⬭ Foundation ch
- - - - Gathering thread

BABY DOLL TOP: BRA CHART

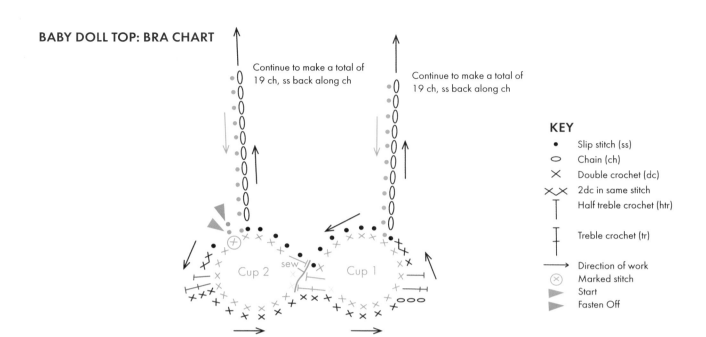

Continue to make a total of 19 ch, ss back along ch

Continue to make a total of 19 ch, ss back along ch

Cup 2   sew   Cup 1

KEY

- • Slip stitch (ss)
- ◯ Chain (ch)
- ✕ Double crochet (dc)
- ✕✕ 2dc in same stitch
- ⊤ Half treble crochet (htr)
- ╪ Treble crochet (tr)
- → Direction of work
- ⊗ Marked stitch
- ▶ Start
- ▶ Fasten Off

BABY DOLL TOP: SKIRT CHART

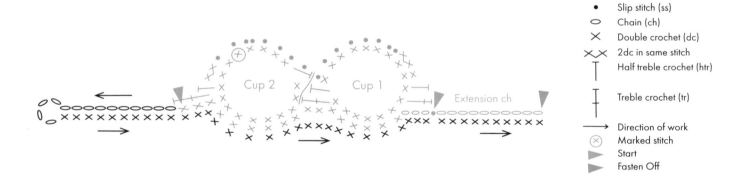

Cup 2   Cup 1   Extension ch

KEY

- • Slip stitch (ss)
- ◯ Chain (ch)
- ✕ Double crochet (dc)
- ✕✕ 2dc in same stitch
- ⊤ Half treble crochet (htr)
- ╪ Treble crochet (tr)
- → Direction of work
- ⊗ Marked stitch
- ▶ Start
- ▶ Fasten Off

CORSET CUPS CHART

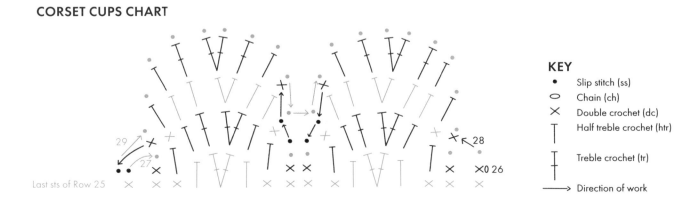

29   28
27   ✕0 26
Last sts of Row 25

KEY

- • Slip stitch (ss)
- ◯ Chain (ch)
- ✕ Double crochet (dc)
- ⊤ Half treble crochet (htr)
- ╪ Treble crochet (tr)
- → Direction of work

HAIR WITH CURLERS DIAGRAM

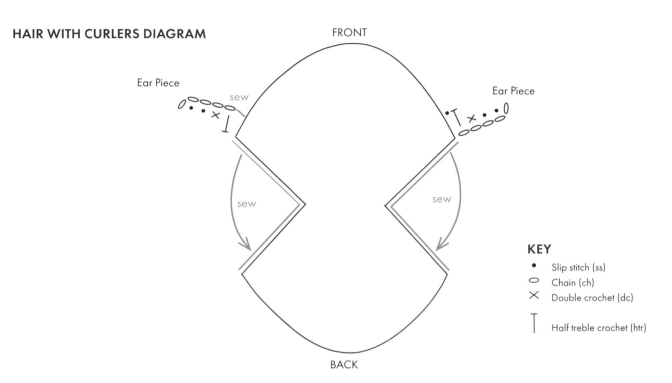

KEY

- • Slip stitch (ss)
- ⌀ Chain (ch)
- ✕ Double crochet (dc)
- ⊤ Half treble crochet (htr)

BABY DOLL PANTS DIAGRAM

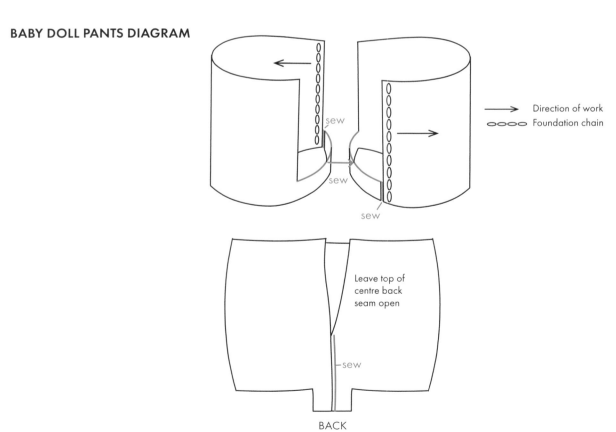

→ Direction of work
ᴓᴓᴓᴓ Foundation chain

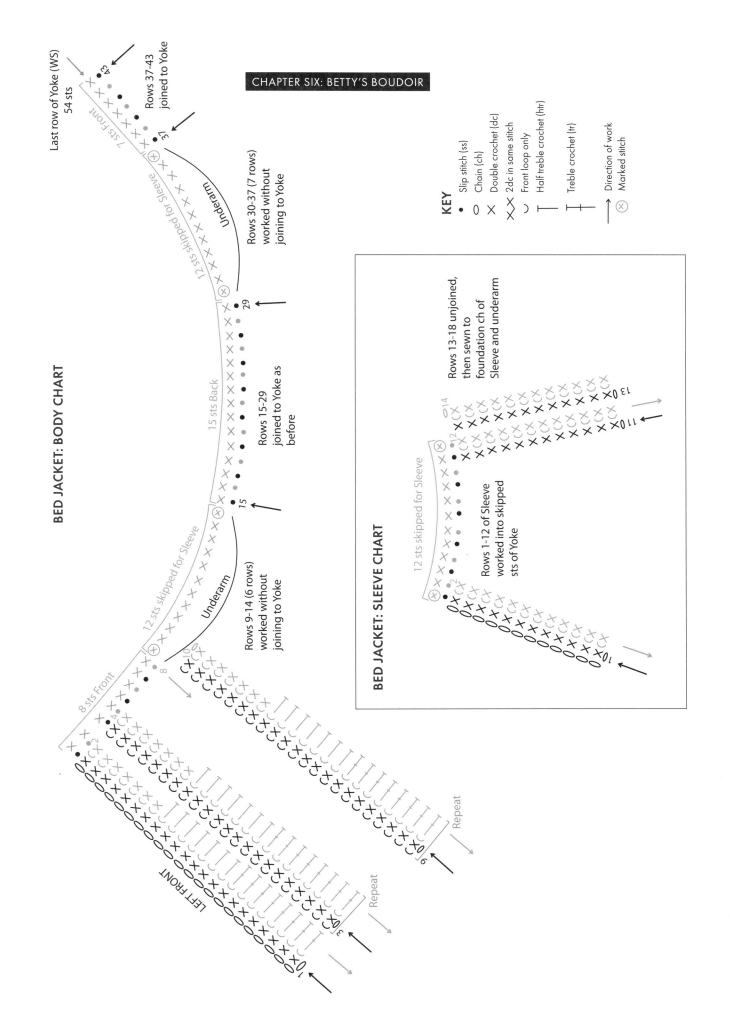

BED JACKET: BODY CHART

Last row of Yoke (WS)
54 sts

Rows 37-43 joined to Yoke

43

37

7 sts Front

12 sts skipped for Sleeve

Underarm

Rows 30-37 (7 rows) worked without joining to Yoke

29

15 sts Back

Rows 15-29 joined to Yoke as before

15

12 sts skipped for Sleeve

Underarm

Rows 9-14 (6 rows) worked without joining to Yoke

8

8 sts Front

10

4

2

LEFT FRONT

Repeat

Repeat

3

1

KEY

• Slip stitch (ss)

◯ Chain (ch)

✕ Double crochet (dc)

✕✕ 2dc in same stitch

◡ Front loop only

⊤ Half treble crochet (htr)

⊥ Treble crochet (tr)

→ Direction of work

⊗ Marked stitch

BED JACKET: SLEEVE CHART

Rows 13-18 unjoined, then sewn to foundation ch of Sleeve and underarm

14

13

11

12 sts skipped for Sleeve

Rows 1-12 of Sleeve worked into skipped sts of Yoke

2

10

ARMHOLE CHART

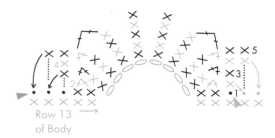

KEY

- • Slip stitch (ss)
- ⬭ Chain (ch)
- ✕ Double crochet (dc)
- ⟩✕ Dc2tog
- ⟶ Direction of work
- ▶ Start
- ▶ Fasten O ff

Shows where st is to
be worked

RED HANDBAG DIAGRAM

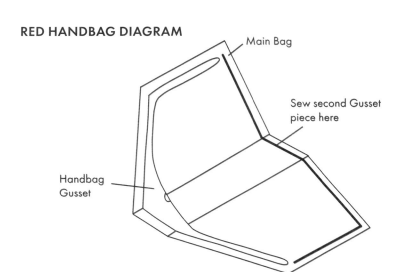

Main Bag

Sew second Gusset
piece here

Handbag
Gusset

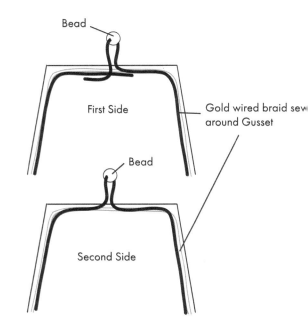

Bead

First Side

Gold wired braid sew
around Gusset

Bead

Second Side

DANCING SHOE DIAGRAM

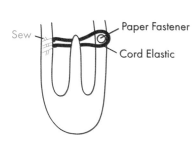

Sew

Paper Fastener

Cord Elastic

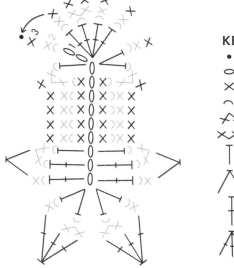

KEY

- • Slip stitch (ss)
- ⬭ Chain (ch)
- ✕ Double crochet (dc)
- ⌒ Back loop only
- ⟩✕ Dc2tog
- ✕✕ 2dc in same st
- T Half treble crochet (htr)
- ⋀ Htr2tog
- ⊤ Treble crochet (tr)
- ⋀ Tr3tog

SHOE CHART

LEOPARD PRINT ILLUSTRATION

Fine Permanent Marker

Yellow Ochre Pencil

LEOPARD PRINT HANDBAG DIAGRAM

Main Bag

Sew second Gusset piece here

Handbag Gusset

First Side

Second Side

Gold wired braid sewn around Gusset

HAT AND HAIR DIAGRAM

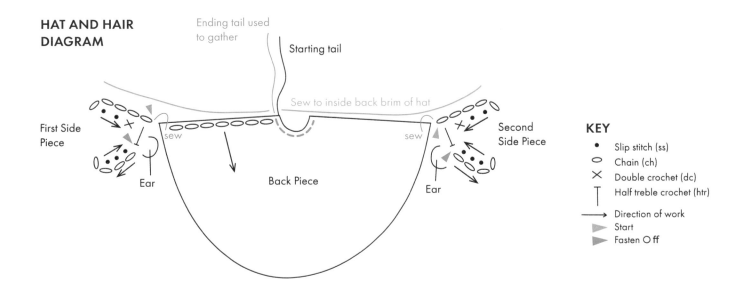

Ending tail used to gather

Starting tail

Sew to inside back brim of hat

First Side Piece

sew

Ear

Back Piece

sew

Ear

Second Side Piece

KEY

• Slip stitch (ss)
◯ Chain (ch)
✕ Double crochet (dc)
⊤ Half treble crochet (htr)
→ Direction of work
▶ Start
▶ Fasten Off

About the author

I've made and drawn things for as long as I can remember, but have been crocheting seriously for about 10 years. I became a technical editor on Simply Crochet magazine when it launched in 2013, and love the geeky side of crochet; patterns, charts, numbers, you name it!

My time is now divided between freelance technical editing and designing. The systematic part of my brain enjoys technical editing, and recently I've had more opportunities to work with designers, teaching them the technical aspects of garment design. I'm also training and mentoring would-be technical editors.

Most of my recent crochet designs have been garments, as I appreciate both the technical and creative challenges involved. I've enjoyed returning to amigurumi, as I've been able to match this with my love of illustration and character creation. It's been a joy to discover Betty and Bert and launch them on some new adventures.

I live in Bristol, with my husband Colin and two sons. Colin and I love travelling, and have a passion for India, having visited several times. Fortunately for me, crochet and travelling go quite well together, as it's such a good thing to do while waiting around. Crochet also goes well with another of my favourite pastimes, which is sitting in cafés drinking coffee. Eating cake is good too, but doesn't go quite as well with crochet!

Acknowledgements

With thanks to everyone who has been part of the production of this book, to Katherine, Jane B and Jesse, Elizabeth and Jane T. Also to Niamh, you were and are amazing! Thanks to my wonderful colleagues at Simply Crochet who have advised, celebrated and propped me up at various stages of the process. Thanks to Scheepjes, for championing and supporting. Hugest thanks to my wonderful family, I love you and am so grateful for you! To my boys, of whom I am so proud, and though wouldn't want to admit it, I know they're proud of me. And to Colin, who has put up with various stages of the 'project Cara' cycle, and is my business manager, friend, and encourager-in-chief. Love you.